Raw Vegan Bodybuilding

How to Gain Muscle and Be Fit On the Raw Food Diet

Sivan Berko

The information in this book is designed for educational purposes only. It is not intended to be a substitute for informed medical advice or care. You should not use this information to diagnose or treat any health problems or illnesses without consulting your pediatrician or family doctor. Please consult a doctor with any questions or concerns you might have regarding your condition.

ISBN: 1506197175
ISBN-13: 978-1506197173

Free E-books Club:

I would like to give you a full access to my VIP club in which you receive FREE E-books on a weekly basis:

Receive Free E-books Here:

http://bit.ly/1DT3SWe

I do this simply because I want my readers to get a lot of value, reach their maximum potential and have a better life. Be the change you want to see in the world!

There is another gift waiting for you at the end of the book.

DEDICATION:

This book is dedicated to those who will never rest until they achieve their goals. To the ones that are aiming to create the best version of themselves. To all the open minded people out there. To the ones that are willing to open their heart and listen, and to all of those people that are being criticized everyday for the way that they live or the road that they have chosen. Never ever settle. People may hate you for being different and not living by society's standards, but deep down, they wish they had the courage to do the same!

WHY I WROTE THIS BOOK?

For as long as I remember myself, I was always into fitness and different types of sports. At the age of 16, I got my first gym membership. The minute I touched the weights, I fell in love.

There was something about training at the gym that got me addicted. As I got some progress, I realized that it is not just about training but also about nutrition and what you put into your body.

I started educating myself with information about nutrition and bodybuilding. I read books, articles, watched videos and even hired coaches and nutrition consultants. I did see results and I learned a lot. I can tell for sure that I got progress and developed a nice muscle mass. As you probably know, the most talked issue about nutrition for bodybuilders and athletes in general is the PROTEIN and the clean eating. Dietitians and nutrition consultant usually talk about, emphasize the protein and overfeed the athletes with loads of animal proteins and products.

I was one of them. I really wanted to get serious, wanted to get into bodybuilding and even compete. My diet was full of proteins, low in carbs. I was eating very clean, following a strict diet. My dietitian allows me one cheat meal every two weeks, but I didn't even think about using this cheat meal, since I wanted results so bad, more than I wanted this cheat meal.

After a couple of month I started to feel weird. I have started to notice changes in my body but also in my overall health. I started suffering from thyroid issues. Discovering later that it has been caused by the loads of animal proteins I was eating. My acne got worth. I felt tired all the time. My asthma and allergies got worse. I was eating healthy (or what I thought/have been taught that was healthy) but I didn't feel healthy at all. My period was gone. I felt like something is wrong. This is not how I am supposed to feel. There was then that I started researching about healthy eating and the effect that the body has on our body. I felt like there is a better solution, there must be another way to train hard, eat healthy and FEEL AMAZING!

It was then that I was introduced to a vegan diet by one of my friends. I was very skeptic about this vegan lifestyle at first. I was so worried that it will affect my training and that I won't get enough protein. I was in doubt. So at the beginning I eliminated meat and dairy products from my diet. It was then that I felt a shift in my health. It was clear that my energy levels were much higher. The asthma and allergies were gone and so was my acne. I still ate fish and eggs though. Loads of them, because that's what I was told. Since I don't eat meat and dairy products I will have to get protein from the other sources so the amounts I ate were still a lot. But I was still suffering from Hypothyroidism and I still haven't got my period. I start to worry. Since I have seen the good influence of eliminating the meat and dairy from my diet, after a couple of month, I decided to eliminate the fish and eggs as well.

I kept reading and educating myself. It bothered me a lot. I wanted to prove that it is possible to build muscle on a vegan diet. There is a lot of protein in plant sources and there is absolutely nothing in animal products that we can't get from plants.

As a vegan I was introduced to new foods like tofu, Seiten, different types of lentils, etc. I was very interested in what's inside my food. As a bodybuilder, you know how it is, you have to check the nutritional value of everything.

And that's where I started researching the ingredients and the processes that my food is going through until it reaches the shelf. It was an eye opener journey. Even the vegan alternatives, I was amazed with all the process that our

"food" in the supermarket is going through. I can't even call it food.

I decided that I want to eat what we are naturally intended to eat - which is raw, organic, fresh, vegan food. Our body was designed to eat certain foods. We are designed to eat what nature gave us with the tools that our body has. Fruits, vegetables, nuts, seeds, legumes.

Our body doesn't recognize all the things that are called "food" in the supermarket. The "food" that is full of chemicals, artificial additives, processed and enriched ingredients. Let alone, empty from essential nutrients. Those enriched ingredients aren't available for the body to absorb. They are not in their natural form.

It was clear that these foods are empty. Dead.

There is nothing efficient when eating dead food.

I started my raw journey ever since and I don't regret for a moment. After a couple of years now on the raw vegan diet, I can tell for sure that this is absolutely the best present I gave to my body. I encourage you to start your journey and experiment for yourself.

I would love to hear your thoughts, answer your questions and help you reach your maximum potential and achieve your goals.

My Facebook page: <u>Sivan Berko</u>

Table of Contents

Introduction

I want to thank you and congratulate you for purchasing this book.

This book contains proven steps and strategies on how to build muscle using a purely raw vegan diet and tested techniques of training.
This book is meant to stimulate THOUGHT in your mind and to open a door for a new road, which is less traveled by most people of today's world.

In this book we get deeper into the 'behind the scenes' factors that are sure to help you gain muscle as well as what to do in order to have a well sculpted physique in the most healthiest, most natural way.

I am going to teach you how to use a raw vegan diet to get all the nutrients you need to bulk up and to be in the best health and shape of your life!

Now, get your notebook ready, you are about to go on a body-building learning journey of your life!

Thanks again for purchasing this book, I hope you enjoy it!

CHAPTER 1

A THREE-PRONGED APPROACH TO MUSCLE BUILDING

YOU ARE WHAT YOU TRAIN

Imagine living in a world where you could wish for anything you have ever desired and bam! You have it! Like waking up to a well toned Hulk-like body! Hmmm...that's just what it is, an imagination.

Back to reality! Muscle building is not for the faint hearted. There is one phrase used in the technology world that I really like to use with reference to our bodies and it goes like this, 'Garbage in Garbage Out.'
If you feed your body with a healthy, raw vegan diet; do all the right exercises in the right way, putting in the required effort and consistency and getting some good rest for your muscles to recover; you are going to be the true definition of a Greek god or goddess!

On the other hand if you feed on junk, go to the gym every once in a blue moon or let me even say go to the gym regularly but execute all the body-building disasters in the book, you are going to be one train wreck!

The most important aspect of bodybuilding and muscle building is consistency. You need to make a commitment to yourself and stick with it. A lot of time to preparing food and weight training go into adding muscle and changing your shape; it is not for the weak at heart. Consistency in eating and weight training are the keys to success.

So, what's the best way to train your body to build muscle? We are going to look at this in two parts; for beginners who are out to build muscle and for the 'veterans' who want to increase their muscle mass.

NEWBIES OUT TO GET SOME MUSCLE

The first thing I can't emphasize more on is that; don't expect to see muscles bulging from your shirt after your first session in the gym! It does take a lot of work to see some muscle definition. Whether it is your first time in the gym or you have been doing this for years and years, for as long as there is no pain, there is not going to be any gain!

Am not trying to scare you or discourage you from training, on the contrary, I am preparing you mentally for what to expect and trust me on this, your best training moment will be that day you look in the mirror and be like, "The man/ lady in the mirror is so damn sexy!"

The good thing about being a newbie at the gym is that you are going to see results much faster compared to someone who has been doing this for a long time. This is because your muscles are not used to any extra activity apart from the usual walking, carrying a box up a flight of stairs and so on; therefore, regular training using minimal weights is going to stimulate your muscle fibers.

With time, you will reach the stagnant stage where muscle growth comes to a standstill. The antidote for this is to increase your weights and at the same time reduce the number of reps. Reducing the number of reps is very important at this juncture as it ensures that you do not weaken your body by overtraining it. We are going to talk more about this later.

I advice newbies to train every 5 -6 times in a week with minimal weights but after a number of months when you don't notice any gain, in addition to increase the amount of weights you lift and the reps you do, I would also advice you to reduce your training days to 4 days in a week so that you give your body enough time to recover.

Changing up your workouts is important. Your body gets used to what it is training. Many newbies fall into a habit of doing exercises they are used to, but you need to change your workouts to accelerate muscle growth. We will get more into that later.

VETERAN TRAINERS

Owing to the fact that you have been training for at least a couple of years now, you are very familiar with the basic training rules and tricks to get a rock solid body. However, there is one mistake that most bodybuilders do unawares; wanting to build muscle and cut at the same time. Don't kill yourself trying to do this, over time; I came to learn that this is impossible, the hard way. The fact is, you can't be on a really low calorie intake and try to build muscle, because then, your muscles won't have enough fuel to recover and grow bigger.

However, I will tell you what is possible; losing fat and building muscle at the same time, well, you probably knew this already.

Building muscle is like pottery. You first have to mould clay (body) into a pot of desired size (muscle) then after that, you can now get into the finer detailing of decorating the pot (defining/ cutting your muscles).

Workouts and training programs are not the same for all individuals or bodies. To find a good workout split (schedule of which body part to train on which day) is to look at what you need to increase the most. Set up your workouts to match your body and what it needs. Place weak body parts in the beginning of your week and non-lagging body parts in the latter part of the week. This will ensure you are training the most needed body parts when you are the most focused and strongest. Example: If your shoulders need to be developed more e than your back, place shoulder training in the early part of the week and back training in the latter part of the week.

We'll talk more about this later. At this stage, your primary concern should be feeding your muscles, stimulating and building your muscles and finally, resting your muscles. This is the perfect muscle growth formula!

YOU ARE WHAT YOU EAT

Nutrition is an integral part of building muscle and you have to be extra careful with everything that goes into your body. The raw vegan diet is the holy grail of diets when it comes to building muscle. It is very clean and equipped with all the essential nutrients that go right into your muscle as well as giving you the energy to be able to train.

One of the very costly mistakes that most people trying to build muscle make is making wrong food choices.

We are still going to apply the 'Garbage in Garbage Out principle' in what we eat. Clean food is a must if you want to see positive results. Dark-green, leafy veggies should feature constantly in your meal plan. They are packed with proteins and other essential nutrients that will help you get bigger muscles and stay healthy at the same time.

Back when I was consuming lots of animal protein in order to bulk up, I had a terrible experience with thyroid issues and as you know, an imbalanced hormonal system means no matter how hard you train, you will not see any significant positive change. The raw vegan diet was a game changer for me and I am now at my best and healthiest shape!

For one, plant based foods have got all the essential nutrients that you need to build all the muscle in the world! Secondly, with a raw vegan diet, it is very easy to maintain a healthy weight and body that is disease free as there is nothing like bad cholesterol or unhealthy fats unlike with an animal-based diet.

You would be very surprised to know that foods like broccoli contain protein. The thing with the raw vegan diet is that you receive first grade nutrition that is in turn reflected in the bulge under your shirt. Another great plus for this diet is that it is very easy to maintain the recommended daily calorie intake as opposed to animal based diets that are high in saturated fats. Chances of ending up with the wrong kind of bulge under your shirt are very high!

We will be looking at the raw vegan diet in detail in the next chapter.

WHAT DO YOU HORMONES HAS TO DO WITH MUSCLE BUILDING?

Metabolism and bodybuilding go hand in hand. A good metabolism means that all your hormones are functioning correctly and are well balanced. Balanced hormones ensure that your muscles are getting the required amount of blood sugar; your insulin levels are stable and that you are burning off energy as you take it in through what you eat.

INCREASED MUSCLE MASS = INCREASED METABOLIC RATE

The time after an intensive workout is when your physiological clock is reset. This is when the used up fat and glucose stores are topped up; torn muscles are repaired and general recovery for all muscles in your body happens. This process is energy intensive meaning that, the more you work your muscles, the more calories you are going to burn post-workout. Particularly for strength training, for as long as you train hard enough, your metabolic rate is going to be faster and better.

When it comes to hormones, there is something you need to watch out for; endocrine disruptors- anything that changes how your hormones should work. The number one endocrine disruptor is anything processed that comes into contact with your body; be it food, lotion, perfume, herbicides, you name it.

HOW DO THESE AFFECT YOUR HORMONES?

Parabens are chemicals that are used as food preservatives as well as in cosmetics due to their efficacy and low cost. Parabens have been found to mimic the hormone estrogen. Additionally, these chemicals interfere with your thyroid, hypothalamus, basically every system in your body.

Once there is an imbalance of hormones of your body, the first thing you will notice is a change in attitude as well as degeneration of muscles. This is the reason I will continue insisting that you only feed on the raw vegan diet making sure you only eat organic food to avoid contact with parabens and other chemicals that are going to cause your hormones to go haywire.

Read all the labels of every product you use and if possible go for only organic products.

CHAPTER 2

MYTH: YOU NEED TO FEED ON LOTS OF ANIMAL PROTEIN FOR YOU TO BULK UP!

Many bodybuilders argue that you need to take lots and lots of protein, preferably animal protein for you to notice a significant growth of your muscles. In actual fact, the only way to seriously gain and build muscle is through training using weights in a progressive manner.

The major reason why most bodybuilders take a lot of protein is because their diets is inefficient and is also insufficient in carbs. Especially cooked proteins, which area heavy burden for the body and are inefficient to use. The protein taken is being digested and broken down into individual amino acids.

Some of those amino acids have the ability to transform into glucose, a process that uses so much energy, and uses this to fuel the body. Any food we eat, whether it is carbohydrates, fat or protein to be utilized by our bodies are converted into glucose. Since carbohydrates are made up of simple sugars, they are turned back to simple sugars on digestion. They are therefore the easiest to convert to fuel. Many of our cells rely on glucose as the primary fuel source. These include brain, blood and nerve cells.

So as you can see, muscle growth is very inefficient when our protein intake is high.

What most people don't understand is that it is not about the amount of protein they consume. In the contrary, it is about the amount of calories throughout the day that matters to grow muscle mass. We'll get into that soon.

Fitness and bodybuilding usually represent a healthy lifestyle. Bodybuilders might look healthy from the outside, but actually their body is crying for help. Putting in all these protein powders and animal products is a disaster.

With animal protein, you cannot ignore the heightened risk of developing cancer owing to the many chemicals and antibiotics that the animals get into contact with before reaching the market. Animal protein also contains a lot of bad cholesterol and saturated fats that may have a negative effect when it comes to building muscle. Too much protein is also bad news for your liver. How is this? Well, the liver cannot breakdown excess protein daily and this can lead to liver failure.

Taking too much protein may lead to increased levels of homocysteine (produced in the metabolization of protein) which increases your risk of getting heart disease.

What about protein powder you ask?

Well, protein powders are highly processed. This process of making protein powders often leaves a highly denatured protein, making it useless. Proteins are heated to the point that our bodies do not recognize it as food. On top of that, many manufactures add synthetic, toxic ingredients to their products such as: Aspartame, Saccharin, fructose, and artificial colors, etc.

You can see all of these on the label.

Why cooked food is a big NO! NO!

The very first time I heard of a raw vegan diet I was a bit confused. I could not fathom the thought of eating a purely raw diet. There were so many questions running through my mind like, how will I get certain nutrients? would my body be able to process all these raw foods? Is raw food not contaminated? And so on.

What I didn't understand at the time was that the cooking process actually damages and degrades food making it less nutritional. We actually create food with a very poor nutritional quality by cooking it in any way – boiling, stewing, frying, baking... you name it.

You have probably heard that when you boil your vegetables, all the nutrients go to the water and this is why you will see so many people reuse this water in their cooking. But even then, how much of the nutrients were able to survive the heat? Had the vegetables not been boiled, then, no nutrients would have been lost in the first place!

Effect of heat on proteins

As we had seen earlier, we only need to take 10% of proteins from our food. First, you need to know that there are two main types of proteins:

- **Fibrous structural proteins** – these are very stable and can stand high heat without their composition being altered.

- **Globular functional proteins** – these use hydrogen bonds to maintain their structure but these bonds are highly fragile and are easily destroyed by heat and high pH.

It goes without saying that cooking proteins destroys the hydrogen bonds of the globular functional proteins and thus denatures them. In lay man's terms, heat deprives proteins of their natural qualities.

Destruction of the hydrogen bonds is just but the start of a chain reaction; what's left of the amino acids, fuses together with other bonds that are resistant to enzymes and thus rendering them unbreakable by the body. This makes the proteins useless as they cannot be used by the body in their current state and worse still, they become toxic to the body.

Since these proteins have a new structure that is foreign to the body, the body treats them as aliens that need to be flushed out. By doing this, your immune system is focused on getting rid of these proteins instead of attending to other areas that genuinely require its attention.

Continued attack of the proteins by the body is one of the reasons why there are so many auto-immune disorders and gastrointestinal disorders because we are eating food in the wrong way. The only way food can be beneficial to our body is if we take it in the right form and the right kind.

As for proteins, the only way that your body can fully utilize this class of food is if they are easily broken down by digestive enzymes. Since the body rejects cooked protein, the only way to attain your daily 10% of protein is by taking your food raw; else, you are going to make your body overwork, as it tries to fight off the food you have eaten instead of fighting real intruders!

Vitamins, minerals and other essential nutrients play a huge role in creating balance in the body's physiological functions. Cooking food leaches away a huge percentage of these nutrients leaving the body exposed due to the deficiency of certain nutrients.

The use of heat can lower the bioavailability of many nutrients, particularly water-soluble nutrients in addition to phytochemicals, unsaturated fatty acids and heart-healthy omega-3 fatty acids, docosahexaenoic acid (DHA) and eicosapentaenoic acid (EPA). In addition, dietary fiber intake may become compromised due to the exposure to heat.

Fruits and vegetables are significantly impacted when cooked as these foods contain a large amount of pigmentation. Three pigment categories include chlorophyll – green; carotenoid – yellow and orange; and two flavonoid groups, anthocyanins – blue, purple or red; and anthoxanthin – white.

Cooking also has the potential to generate undesirable components that are carcinogenic. A common compound is nitrosamine. This compound is commonly generated due to the charring, smoking and frying of food.

When carbohydrates are overcooked, a carcinogen, acrylamide, may be generated due to the Maillard Reaction, according to the Journal of Cancer Epidemiology, Biomarkers and Prevention. This leads to an increased risk for certain cancers, such as endometrial and ovarian cancer in postmenopausal women. Acrylamide is present when carbohydrate rich foods are cooked to an internal temperature of 250 degrees Fahrenheit or higher. The longer carbohydrate-rich foods are cooked and the higher the temperature, the greater the amount of acrylamide will occur. For example, breads or overcooked baked potatoes may likely contain acrylamide.

Supplements?

The use of multivitamins is increasing at an exceeding rate today as over $28 billion dollars are spent yearly and will continue to increase. Almost half of Americans, approximately 40 percent, are currently taking a multivitamin, according to Annals of Internal Medicine Editorial, 2013. Americans are living in a society of convenience and are looking quick fixes for their health problems. The FDA does not regulate supplements, and health claims are quite misleading to consumers. In addition, the lack education on supplementations makes it challenging to navigate the supplement section.

Multivitamins and isolated supplements provide little to no benefit in the prevention of disease and cancer or offer any pronounced health benefits. In fact, supplementation may do more harm than good. For example, calcium supplementation studies from the National Institute of Health suggest that calcium supplementation for women and men may increase the risk of heart attack or stroke through calcification of the arteries or plaque buildup. Whole food sources of calcium, including green leafy vegetables, sprouts, and nuts, can offer calcium in a highly bioavailable form.

In addition, the United States Preventive Task Force has found no benefit in postmenopausal women who take regular calcium and vitamin D supplementation for the prevention of fractures. The Western Diet today has caused an imbalance in calcium and magnesium intake. With excessive supplementation of calcium and low magnesium intake, calcium supplementation may not be fully utilized in the body. By consuming a raw vegan diet with whole foods that are rich in magnesium (e.g., fruits, nuts, seeds, sprouts, vegetables), calcium can be adequately stored in the body and prevent health problems, including osteoporosis, arthritis, migraines and premenstrual symptoms.

Over 200 epidemiological studies have shown that consuming wholesome, nutrient dense foods, including fruits, vegetables and fibrous foods, offers superior health benefits than isolated vitamins in supplement form. The body was designed to consume whole food sources, not synthesized vitamins, which are essentially foreign to the human body. In clinical trials, vitamin A and vitamin E taken in vitamin form in higher quantities was linked to a reduction in bone density and hip fracture and hemorrhagic stroke, respectively.

The take away message is the Raw Vegan diet contains all the wholesome foods necessary that work synergistically to offer protection to chronic diseases and cancers while isolated synthesized vitamins at this time do not offer this protection based on clinical trials.

Now let's talk about protein powders. They are becoming increasingly popular today, but the main question is, are they necessary? It is rare for humans to be deficient in protein. Adult women need on average 46 grams per day and men need about 56 grams per day. By eating a variety from each food group, including adequate fruits, vegetables, sprouts and seeds, protein needs will likely be met if not exceeded.

Many whole food protein choices are comprised of high biologically active protein with optimal nutrient-density and flavor. Isolated protein powders lack other healthful nutrients which are present in a variety of whole food sources. This may result in a lack of satiety due to the absence of nutrients in protein powders. Additionally, many protein powders contain artificial ingredients, chemicals and refined sugar, which do not support a healthy lifestyle.

People should focus on consuming whole protein foods throughout the day for optimal digestion and absorption while avoiding the reliance on powders.

Don't think that just because you take supplements means that you are getting the ideal amount of nutrients every day. No! Our bodies are meant to process whole and natural foods. You do not expect to separate vitamins from living enzymes in food and expect them to function in the same way. A raw vegan diet is the only way to reap all the benefits of the food you take and this will provide your body with first grade fuel, allowing you to train optimally.

Complete Proteins

The building blocks of complete proteins are made up of amino acids. We know them as 20 amino acids; 10 are thought to be the most essential since the body cannot create them on its own. For this reason, one receives these amino acids externally-- through food.

These amino acids are found in the highest concentrations in the following animal proteins: meat, fish, eggs, etc.

It is generally believed that these animal proteins are complete proteins of the greatest biological value. Because of this conventional assumption, most of the plant proteins are not considered to be "complete protein."

In understanding things we are deceived because according to common thought, it is not the existence of amino acids in proteins that determines their biological value, rather it is their concentration. What I am trying to say is that with that assumption, even if a certain type of food contains all the amino acids but only in small concentrations it cannot be considered a protein with full biological value. In this orthotropic assumption, this misunderstanding is misleading at its core.

I determine here that it is absolutely certain that a person who eats fruits and vegetables, different nuts and seeds (sesame seeds, sunflower seeds, etc.) receives more than enough of the essential amino acids, which are important for maintaining and building up the body.

It is true that not every plant form contains all the essential amino acids in high concentrations. However, high concentration is not required.

He who feeds himself wisely does not eat only one kind of food for an extended period of time. He eats many different kinds of things, all complementing each other. What isn't found in one food is certainly found in the other. And from all his nourishment as a whole, he will receive all the amino acids in abundance. The same goes for vitamins, minerals, fats and carbohydrates.

There are fruits that are not rich in vitamin A, and there are fruits that are not great sources of vitamin C or B. But one thing is clear-- the one who eats melon , carrots, parsley, citrus fruits, guavas, sunflower seeds, sesame seeds, almonds and other plants will receive plenty of vitamins A, B, and C and will receive all the different kinds of essential amino acids.

Let us open our eyes and see what is the animals' "secret of success" in producing complete proteins in their meat.

The ox and the lamb, the gazelle and the deer-- they do not eat proteins from the animal kingdom ("biologically complete proteins"). These animals are satisfied with the following plant foods. These animals graze in the fields; there they obtain the "plants of the field" -- varying kinds of grass. These grasses have very weak concentrations of amino acids. But since these animals do not restrict themselves to just one type of grass-- they eat many different kinds-- and eat them in sufficient quantities, they receive all the amino acids, which create protein in their meat, where amino acids are found even more than in the grass they eat. This grass, of course, served these animals as the source for their complete protein production-- their meat. This is the nature of things.

The human body functions in a similar way. The human body builds its proteins depending on the unique needs of the individual. Therefore, it is desirable to provide the body with a lot of variation in its diet-- all kinds of fruits and vegetables, nuts and seeds, etc.-- so that the body can obtain all that is necessary for its healthy existence.

Man's fatal mistake is using animal meat to get amino acids. Let us not forget that the proteins that man gets along with his food are not absorbed in their actual form. Instead, they are being broken down into amino acids and then the liver uses them to build many important proteins in our body.

The breaking down of proteins in the body involves exploiting the body's energy. If a person eats concentrated proteins from living beings, he is imposing a great burden on his digestive system, particularly on the liver. Sometimes this burden is truly unbearable. By all accounts, the biological value of meadows grass is less than that of fruits and nuts. So it should be clear that he who takes in animal protein is really just taking in the protein from the meadow grass that the animal ate. The animal creates the protein in its meat from the grass it grazes. Conversely, the person who feeds himself with fruits, vegetables and nuts is consuming excellent sources of protein, since all the amino acids produced in them is found in an ideal manner.

Is there enough protein in the raw vegan diet?

You are probably asking yourself: "Well I am training very heavy and hard to build muscle, don't I have to start consuming more protein? Because protein is used to build muscle"
Well you are not alone. A lot of people are concern about this issue.

Now Let's think about it, when in your life, from the moment you are born to the moment that you die, do you think you are doing the most growth - the most building of muscles and body tissues?

If you said when you are a baby then you are correct. The most growth we experience is in the first year and a half. The first year and a half of your life, that's when you are doing the most explosive growth that you'll ever do. So that's when you are going to need proportionally the most protein that you'll ever need.

Now, what are you eating when you are at this age?
The answer is mother's milk. So how much protein is in mother's milk?

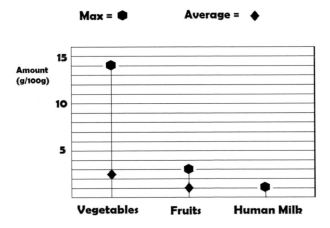

Protein Content:

Max = ●   Average = ◆

32

As you can see, the amount of protein in human milk and the amount of protein in fruit is about the same. So, in fact there can be more protein in fruits and vegetables than in mother's milk.

But as an adult, we finish growing. Now we are just doing maintaining, so why would we need more protein than a baby needs?

So as long as you are not cooking the protein that you are consuming, there is plenty in fruits, vegetables, sprouts and seeds to build all the muscles that you need to build

Let us now look at the 80/10/10 diet and why it is the surest way to gain solid, fibrous muscle.

The 80/10/10 rule

I started on the 80/10/10 diet when I started having some health issues. At first I was a bit skeptical due the fact that I used to eat loads and loads of animal protein before and didn't see how this diet would help me bulk up but to my surprise I had so much more energy to train, the energizer bunny was no match for me! As for the muscle gain, I only have one word, INSANE!

I know your number one question at this point is, **"What is the 80/10/10 diet?"**

First, 80/10/10 stands for 80% carbs, 10% protein and 10% fat. Dr. Douglas M. Graham is the man behind this diet and believes that the above proportions are ideal for stabilized sugar, weight management, athletic ability and body building - this diet creates the optimal environment for increased delivery of oxygen to the cells.

Now that we have answered that question, let us now investigate whether 10% of protein is enough for a bodybuilder like you.

To start with, you should know that all plant based foods contain protein. Many bodybuilders always aim to take all the essential proteins daily but is this really necessary to worry about it?

Food is not the only source of protein. You will be amazed to discover that our bodies usually recycle about 100 grams to 300 grams of our very own protein on a daily basis. This is because our bodies contain a pool of amino acids where new proteins are built. We usually add to this pool by processing the proteins we eat and the proteins in our bodies. This is to say that it is very easy for us to meet all our protein requirements on a raw vegan diet. Raw vegetables especially have high protein content ranging between 10-30%. So, we certainly don't need to take all the essential proteins in one day. With an addition of fruits and a few nuts or seeds we reach to the most logical and efficient diet on the planet.

Take a look at the gorillas for example. They eat fruit, leafs, stalks and some other plants. This guy here weighs 220kg of muscles. It doesn't look like he needs any other protein sources and definitely not from animal products!

If you are still in doubt, ask yourself why you have never heard of chimps needing more protein yet they are very strong and are able to swing from tree to tree on a purely vegan diet.

Plant based protein is all you need for normal function of the body and the fact that the minerals you get from plants are mostly alkaline is more the reason you should take a raw vegan diet.

In summary, when you are on a diet of fruits and veggies alone, your average daily protein consumption is going to be around 5-10%of calories, give or take. A small serving of nuts and seeds is one way to increase your protein intake. My advice to you if you are serious about gaining muscle is that you cannot afford to shrug off the 80/10/10 diet for the healthiest and most efficient way to build muscle.

Gain boundless energy, mass and muscle with the raw vegan diet

Did you know that a chimpanzee is five times stronger than the average man? Is it because they feed on lots and lots of animal protein? Hell no! These apes that bear so much resemblance to man feed on a purely raw vegan diet. So imagine you feeding on a raw vegan diet and combining this with weight lifting; you are definitely going to turn heads around every time you walk down the street, and is that not what you want?

The fact that more and more bodybuilders and athletes swear by the raw vegan 80/10/10 rule now more than ever tells you there is something special about this diet. Let me break it down even further for you.

Scientists over time have come to the conclusion that carbs, proteins and fats are all very essential for good health. However, the portions are what make or break the body's optimal performance. As we had seen earlier, failure to take in enough carbs leads to protein being converted to carbs which is a very energy intensive process. If you are a bodybuilder, this is definitely the last thing you want. Proteins and fats are both very important but they should be taken in small portions for them to be well utilized by the body.

The raw vegan diet is the perfect diet for you if you are looking to bulk up, have lots of energy, stay disease free and be in the best health and shape of your life. Now tell me, what else would you want? I am going to share with you a guideline just to give you an idea of what you should be eating. Note that this is not as rigid as brick and mortar; feel free to alter it to suit your flavors but remember to only include foods that are purely raw and vegan plus watch out for the amount of calories!

Optimal Amount of Calories

How many calories do you need on daily basis? Under the presumption that you are pushing your body to extreme, this will definitely lift the fog:

- On your working day, you need 20 calories per pound of your body weight;

- On your non-working day, you need 17 calories per pound of your body weight.

Many factors, including weight, age, gender and activity level, determine the amount of calories needed per day. The use of an online calculator can give you a rough estimate; however, you can determine how many estimated calories you burn daily and then add on average anywhere between 250 to 500 calories daily. Now it's easy for you to calculate your daily needs. But, you won't import all of your daily calories needs in 2 3 meals. You will spread that amount on 6 or even more daily meals, but with 80-10-10 rule on your mind from now on, right?

As we already discussed it, you need three critical elements: *proteins, fats* and *carbohydrates.*

Proteins are the building blocks of your body and are found in every type of living being on this planet - viruses are nothing more than an advanced form of protein. They are essential for growth of the muscles.

Fats and carbohydrates are main energy sources. When practicing a raw vegan diet the 90% of all fats will be the quality OMEGA-3 and OMEGA-6 fats. This means that your body will metabolize all of the important fats and won't store anything as what is the case with saturated fats coming from animal sources.

The source of mono-unsaturated fats in raw vegan diet comes from nuts, seeds and avocados, but it is easy to control the amounts due to the fact that there is a precise overview for each raw ingredient of vegan diet and the most of it will be metabolized by your body because they are not cooked or heated in any way.

Regular and controlled intake of mono -unsaturated fats ensures high levels of testosterone - critical for strength and muscular growth.

Now, many run from carbs like there's some voodoo magic involved, but as I've explained, your body simply loves sugars (glucose) as it is the most effective way for it to produce energy for every single cell in your body.

You need to understand that your body is not a stationery object. While proteins are building blocks, you need energy in a form of carbohydrates along with additional source: fats. Grasp that your body fancy carbs more than anything else and it is counterproductive to avoid them.

But to fully understand the importance of the carbohydrates intake, here is a quick insight:

- Carbohydrates are most easily transformed into the energy (fuel) desperately needed by every cell of your body; hence every organ, tissue, blood compounds, everything!

- Carbs are stored within the muscle tissue and liver (in a form of a glycogen) to be used later on, in case of an emergency. When you are in the middle of high intensity training, your muscles will burn additional fuel from stored glycogen reserves.

- All studies made to this day point that human body needs at least 60% ratio of carbohydrates in daily calories intake. That's minimum.

Low levels of glycogen in your muscles will result in fatigue and you will not be able to perform tasks that demand high energy output. But there is yet another downside of this situation: as your muscles cannot use the stored glycogen, they will turn to proteins. <u>Your body will metabolize proteins to produce energy</u>!

How this occurs?

When you deprive your body from carbohydrates, your overall glucose level is dropping. Your brain reacts in nanosecond, trying to compensate with stored glycogen. As there is none, it will force-produce it from proteins and fat, because right level of glucose is essential for your survival.

As it is easier for your body to metabolize proteins to get the needed energy, your body will start to "eat" your muscular tissue as the richest reservoir of the proteins. You are guessing the end result.

Even if you try to eat additional doses of proteins, that won't yield any results due to the low levels or total lack of carbohydrates in your diet and in your system which already altered the way your proteins are metabolized.

You want slow digesting carbs throughout the day as they won't cause the insulin peaks resulting in fat storing.

Another thing to consider is the time of the day when you train. You need to adjust your daily diet according to your training habits/schedule. Don't worry, I have you covered. Read on.

Pre-workout nutrition

If you want to train at your peak and get the most from your gym sessions, quality fuel for your muscles is critical. Your main aim should be to utilize every single gram of the carbs you take either as immediate fuel or to restore the used up glucose stores. Only eat what you need, going overboard will mean stored fats.

So, the meal before your workout should be high in carbs. You will want to give your body at least an hour for the carbs to be digested and go to your blood stream ensuring that your glucose stores are full before training.

Critical thing to do and the very first thing you need to do when you wake up in the morning is to import fast-digesting carbs into your system. Over the night, you glucose level dropped significantly and your body was using stored glycogen.

This action will peak the insulin level and start the overall metabolizing process to dispatch required glucose directly into your cells, while storing the rest. If you fail to do this, your body will supply cells with energy coming from a different source! and you want to avoid this.

An hour before your training session you need to import high-octane food consisting of carbs, proteins and fats.

Post-workout nutrition

Within the hour after your training session (preferably right after it), you should import a combination of proteins and carbohydrates to help the recovery process of your muscular tissue. Failing to do so will yield none of the results in muscle gain.

To some extent, you understand the main mechanisms behind muscular growth and energy metabolism processes. But to fully grasp the importance of the post-workout nutrition you need to know how your body will make your muscle bigger than it has been so far.

The mechanism behind this magic is simple: when you overload your muscle fiber, it snaps. As a precaution, your body will create 2 for each snapped.

And it can only do that if it has all needed resources: proteins, fats and carbs.

Studies have shown that 2 hours after the extensive workout is too late to properly initiate this healing process, so you better do it fast - within 30 minutes after your workout.

How much? 0,5 grams of carbohydrates per pound of your total body weight. By using 80-10-10 principle, you can easily calculate the amount of proteins and fat.

Protein is a very essential nutrient for muscle growth and repair, but not in the amounts that we have been previously taught. When protein is in the raw, pure form, the quantities do not need be as high and our system won't need to overwork. It is therefore very important to eat quality proteins at this point. Don't forget your leafy greens as they are the best protein sources!
Lettuce/spinach/kale/collard greens/parsley/dill/coriander etc.

Planning your meals

Daily meal plan examples:

(Broken down for both morning and evening training schedules)

Meal plan 1:

Morning Workout Schedule

The first meal of the day should be very refreshing and provide you with enough energy to start of your day.

If you work out in the morning, this should be the pre-workout meal (more on pre-workout nutrition is discussed later on). Eat your pre-workout meal approximately an hour before you start your training, in order to give it some time to digest—any food left churning in your stomach can cause blood to be diverted from the muscles you're training, harming your workout (if you still feel like the meal hasn't settled after an hour, wait a little longer before training).

Meal #1 - immediately after you wake up - *Pre-workout meal*

You can start your day with fruits with high water content like: watermelon, cantaloupe, grape, etc.
I like to cut a watermelon and eat it with a spoon.

If you don't feel like eating a watermelon or if it's just not available at this time of the year (seasonal

availability), your breakfast can also be a smoothie featuring whole fruits (around 4 pieces of whole fruit + 12 ounces of water, you can also add a handful of leafy greens).
For example:

- 3-4 Bananas, 2 persimmons, lettuce
  or
  2 apples, 2 pears, kale leaves or
  3-4 oranges, Handful of strawberries, celery sticks

  Let your creative juices flow but make sure everything is raw and vegan.

Meal #2 - *Post-workout meal*

- 0.5 liter of raw fresh squeezed fruit juice, raw vegan lettuce wraps filled with fruits or vegetables

Meal #3

- 5-6 pieces of whole fruits, celery sticks

Meal#4

- Large bowl of raw zucchini pasta with raw tomato sauce

Meal #5

- Handful of nuts/ ⅓of Avocado / Handful of seeds

Green salad made from spinach, broccoli, zucchini, and cabbage, coriander with salsa dressing (mango, peppers, basil, onion, and lemon juice), 12 ounces of water

Meal #6 - *Dinner*

- Large vegetable salad with a variety of greens Bowl of sprouted mung beans/ adzuki beans/ chickpea

Meal plan 2:

Evening Workout Schedule

Meal #1 - *Breakfast - Immediately after you wake up*

- 4 pieces of whole fruit + 12 ounces of water/coconut water

Meal #2 - *An hour after the Breakfast 1*

- 1 head of lettuce, half of kale and 3 oranges

Meal #3

- Large vegetables salad with kale, pine nuts, peppers, cucumbers and tomatoes, smoothie made from apples, carrots and spinach, 16 ounces of water

Meal #4 - *Pre-workout meal* - an hour before your training

- Green Smoothie – Made from 2-3 pieces of whole fruit and leafy greens

Meal #5 - *Post-workout meal*

- Large green salad with walnuts and pecans and mixed vegetables, collard green wraps with peppers, 16 ounces of water

Meal #6 - *Dinner*

- Romaine hearts and salsa green salad with spinach, broccoli, zucchini, and cabbage; Bowl of *sprouted legumes: beans / lentils.

Don't worry, I've provided you with detailed insights of sprouts, their usage and how-to-sprout guide.

Additional Dietary Guidelines

Things to Remember:
- Greens! Greens! Greens! Go eat your greens!

- Sprouts are great protein sources as well, better be eaten in the evening because they take longer to digest than fruits and vegetables so in order to avoid digestion problems, it is better to eat them last in your day.

- Nuts and seeds contain a nice amount of protein, but they contain lots of fat, so you should be careful with those.

- Carbs are important for post workout as they top up the used up glucose stores and also maximize recovery. Whole fruits and vegetables will be your best choice in order to maximize your recovery! It is also best to eat the high-calorie fruits in the morning, since the body is calorie-deprived after the night of sleeping. Glucose tolerance is typically at its highest during the morning.

Go ahead and do a complete overhaul of your kitchen and replace everything with fresh, organic raw fruits, vegetables, nuts and seeds and watch yourself become stronger by the day!

Generally, your daily caloric intake depends on your training intensity and your daily activities. Obviously if you are a very active person, and you want to gain muscle, you will need to eat more!

I suggest using cronometer in order to see where you are with your calories (you can put your height, weight, and your goal – in this case gaining weight, and it will tell you exactly how many calories you need according to your goal).

I used cronometer in order to calculate the amount of calories and nutrients I consume. It can really serve as an eye-opener and show you that we have lots of nutrients we didn't know of, in lots of vegetables and fruits, like omega-3, protein, etc. just try it yourself https://cronometer.com

Using cronometer will also help you learn how many calories each fruit contains. In time, it will be very easy for you to know exactly how many pieces of fruit you need or how big your salad/smoothie/meal needs to be.

Here is the nutritional information of some of the common foods in the raw vegan diet:

Nutrition information	Protein	Fat	Carbs	Calories
1 raw, romaine lettuce head	7.7g	1.9g	20.6g	106.4
250g, raw cauliflower	4.8g	0.7g	12.4g	62.5
250g, raw spinach	7.2g	1g	9.1g	57.5
1 cup, walnuts	18g	76g	16g	765
1 medium banana	1.3g	0.4g	27g	105
250g raw, kale	10.7g	2.3g	21.9 g	122.5
250g, broccoli	7.1g	0.9g	16.6g	85
165g pineapple chunks	1g	0g	22g	83
1 raw mango	3g	1g	50g	202
1 cup, raw celery	1g	0g	3g	16
1 medium cucumber	2g	0.3g	10.9g	48.2

Check out those next few pages. I don't think you have anything to worry about.

The following section contains combinations of tables with a nutrient composition of some of the most used.

250g kale, raw

General		
Energy	122.5 kcal	6%
Alcohol	0.0 g	No Target
Caffeine	0.0 mg	No Target
Water	210.1 g	8%

Carbohydrates		
Carbs	21.9 g	6%
Fiber	9.0 g	36%
Starch	7.2 g	No Target
Sugars	5.7 g	No Target

Lipids		
Fat	2.3 g	11%
Monounsaturated	0.1 g	No Target
Polyunsaturated	0.8 g	No Target
Omega-3	0.5 g	41%
Omega-6	0.3 g	3%
Saturated	0.2 g	1%
Trans-Fats	0.0 g	n/a
Cholesterol	0.0 mg	0%

Protein		
Protein	10.7 g	11%
Cystine	0.1 g	47%
Histidine	0.2 g	33%
Isoleucine	0.5 g	47%
Leucine	0.6 g	28%
Lysine	0.5 g	31%
Methionine	0.1 g	14%
Phenylalanine	0.4 g	64%
Threonine	0.4 g	47%
Tryptophan	0.1 g	47%
Tyrosine	0.3 g	45%
Valine	0.5 g	33%

1 medium banana

General		
Energy	105.0 kcal	5%
Alcohol	0.0 g	No Target
Caffeine	0.0 mg	No Target
Water	88.4 g	3%

Carbohydrates		
Carbs	27.0 g	8%
Fiber	3.1 g	12%
Starch	6.3 g	No Target
Sugars	14.4 g	No Target

Lipids		
Fat	0.4 g	2%
Monounsaturated	0.0 g	No Target
Polyunsaturated	0.1 g	No Target
Omega-3	0.0 g	3%
Omega-6	0.1 g	0%
Saturated	0.1 g	1%
Trans-Fats	0.0 g	n/a
Cholesterol	0.0 mg	0%

Protein		
Protein	1.3 g	1%
Cystine	0.0 g	5%
Histidine	0.1 g	17%
Isoleucine	0.0 g	3%
Leucine	0.1 g	4%
Lysine	0.1 g	4%
Methionine	0.0 g	2%
Phenylalanine	0.1 g	9%
Threonine	0.0 g	4%
Tryptophan	0.0 g	5%
Tyrosine	0.0 g	2%
Valine	0.1 g	4%

250g broccoli, raw

General		
Energy	85.0 kcal	4%
Alcohol	0.0 g	No Target
Caffeine	0.0 mg	No Target
Water	223.3 g	8%

Carbohydrates		
Carbs	16.6 g	5%
Fiber	6.5 g	26%
Starch	5.9 g	No Target
Sugars	4.3 g	No Target

Lipids		
Fat	0.9 g	4%
Monounsaturated	0.0 g	No Target
Polyunsaturated	0.1 g	No Target
Omega-3	0.1 g	5%
Omega-6	0.0 g	0%
Saturated	0.1 g	0%
Trans-Fats	0.0 g	n/a
Cholesterol	0.0 mg	0%

Protein		
Protein	7.1 g	7%
Cystine	0.1 g	33%
Histidine	0.1 g	28%
Isoleucine	0.2 g	19%
Leucine	0.3 g	16%
Lysine	0.3 g	21%
Methionine	0.1 g	18%
Phenylalanine	0.3 g	44%
Threonine	0.2 g	28%
Tryptophan	0.1 g	39%
Tyrosine	0.1 g	19%
Valine	0.3 g	23%

250g cauliflower, raw

General		
Energy	62.5 kcal	3%
Alcohol	0.0 g	No Target
Caffeine	0.0 mg	No Target
Water	230.2 g	9%

Carbohydrates		
Carbs	12.4 g	4%
Fiber	5.0 g	20%
Starch	2.7 g	No Target
Sugars	4.8 g	No Target

Lipids		
Fat	0.7 g	3%
Monounsaturated	0.0 g	No Target
Polyunsaturated	0.0 g	No Target
Omega-3	0.0 g	2%
Omega-6	0.0 g	0%
Saturated	0.2 g	1%
Trans-Fats	0.0 g	n/a
Cholesterol	0.0 mg	0%

Protein		
Protein	4.8 g	5%
Cystine	0.1 g	24%
Histidine	0.1 g	26%
Isoleucine	0.2 g	17%
Leucine	0.3 g	13%
Lysine	0.5 g	34%
Methionine	0.1 g	9%
Phenylalanine	0.2 g	25%
Threonine	0.2 g	24%
Tryptophan	0.1 g	24%
Tyrosine	0.1 g	19%
Valine	0.3 g	23%

1 medium cucumber

General		
Energy	48.2 kcal	2%
Alcohol	0.0 g	No Target
Caffeine	0.0 mg	No Target
Water	286.6 g	11%

Carbohydrates		
Carbs	10.9 g	3%
Fiber	2.2 g	9%
Starch	2.5 g	No Target
Sugars	5.0 g	No Target

Lipids		
Fat	0.3 g	2%
Monounsaturated	0.0 g	No Target
Polyunsaturated	0.1 g	No Target
Omega-3	0.0 g	1%
Omega-6	0.1 g	1%
Saturated	0.1 g	1%
Trans-Fats	0.0 g	n/a
Cholesterol	0.0 mg	0%

Protein		
Protein	2.0 g	2%
Cystine	0.0 g	6%
Histidine	0.0 g	6%
Isoleucine	0.1 g	6%
Leucine	0.1 g	4%
Lysine	0.1 g	5%
Methionine	0.0 g	3%
Phenylalanine	0.1 g	9%
Threonine	0.1 g	7%
Tryptophan	0.0 g	7%
Tyrosine	0.0 g	5%
Valine	0.1 g	5%

1 head of romaine lettuce

General		
Energy	106.4 kcal	5%
Alcohol	0.0 g	No Target
Caffeine	0.0 mg	No Target
Water	592.3 g	22%

Carbohydrates		
Carbs	20.6 g	6%
Fiber	13.1 g	53%
Starch	0.0 g	No Target
Sugars	7.4 g	No Target

Lipids		
Fat	1.9 g	9%
Monounsaturated	0.1 g	No Target
Polyunsaturated	1.0 g	No Target
Omega-3	0.7 g	64%
Omega-6	0.3 g	3%
Saturated	0.2 g	1%
Trans-Fats	0.0 g	n/a
Cholesterol	0.0 mg	0%

Protein		
Protein	7.7 g	8%
Cystine	0.0 g	18%
Histidine	0.1 g	25%
Isoleucine	0.3 g	27%
Leucine	0.5 g	23%
Lysine	0.4 g	25%
Methionine	0.1 g	18%
Phenylalanine	0.4 g	61%
Threonine	0.3 g	34%
Tryptophan	0.1 g	30%
Tyrosine	0.2 g	24%
Valine	0.3 g	25%

250g spinach, raw

General		
Energy	57.5 kcal	3%
Alcohol	0.0 g	No Target
Caffeine	0.0 mg	No Target
Water	228.5 g	8%

Carbohydrates		
Carbs	9.1 g	3%
Fiber	5.5 g	22%
Starch	2.5 g	No Target
Sugars	1.1 g	No Target

Lipids		
Fat	1.0 g	4%
Monounsaturated	0.0 g	No Target
Polyunsaturated	0.4 g	No Target
Omega-3	0.3 g	31%
Omega-6	0.1 g	1%
Saturated	0.2 g	1%
Trans-Fats	0.0 g	n/a
Cholesterol	0.0 mg	0%

Protein		
Protein	7.2 g	7%
Cystine	0.1 g	41%
Histidine	0.2 g	30%
Isoleucine	0.4 g	35%
Leucine	0.6 g	27%
Lysine	0.4 g	27%
Methionine	0.1 g	25%
Phenylalanine	0.3 g	49%
Threonine	0.3 g	38%
Tryptophan	0.1 g	46%
Tyrosine	0.3 g	41%
Valine	0.4 g	29%

Sprouts

Research has confirmed that certain foods, such as seeds and legumes are highly nutritious; however, what may be lacking is the bioavailability of the nutrients to the human body due to inadequate digestion of nutrients, leading in poor absorption and uptake at the cellular level. Each of these foods contains an enzyme inhibitor or barrier, e.g., tannins, phytic acid, which interfere in the absorption of the nutrients in these foods. For example, if a person consumed flax seeds without milling them first, there will be no nutritional benefit due to the lack of bioavailability in the whole seed.

The solution to this inhibition problem is through sprouting, which involves making enzymes to help break down the nutrients into a highly absorbable form. Essentially, the sprouting process activates the seed and leads to bioavailability and heightened nutrient absorption.

When flaxseed is sprouted, its nutrient availability increases up to 600% compared to unsprouted flaxseed; this all occurs do the germination process. People are exposed to high levels of free radical damage daily, including stress, pollution, high traffic, processed foods and medication; sprouting can almost double the antioxidant radical absorbance capacity, which results in greater antioxidant absorption from beta-carotene, various vitamins and lycopene, which will help to neutralize the free radical more efficiently.

When seeds and legumes are germinated or sprouted, phytic acid or an inhibitor will be reduced, allowing greater digestion of these proteins. This may help heal the gut, as there will be less inflammation thus improved gastrointestinal health.

Overall, many benefits occur from sprouting:

- Simple sugars are formed from starch breakdown for easier digestion

- Efficient breakdown of protein to amino acids

- Efficient breakdown of fats to fatty acids

- Higher levels of vitamins and minerals in the body

- Antioxidant levels up to 100% higher, resulting in less free radical accumulation

- Higher enzymatic activity

- Fewer toxins in the body

- Higher anticancer compounds

- Maximized bioavailability of nutrients for optimal health

There are some easy methods for sprouting foods. Let's take for example Mung beans and lentils. When lentils are sprouted, this results in improved digestion, less gas and increased vitamin absorption. These benefits are derived due to the neutralization of phytic acid in lentils, resulting in better digestion of vitamins and minerals.

Lentils Sprouting

All you need:

Lentils, 2/3 c.

Mason Jar, 1 quart or a Kitchen Seed Sprouter

Water, 2 c.

Cheesecloth, 3-4

All you do:

Add 2/3 c. dry lentils in a 1 quart- mason jar. Fill with 2 c. water and let sit overnight or for 8-12 hours. This will result in swelling of the lentils.

Add thin cheesecloth on top of the jar to allow some air to seep through.

Simply drain the water from the jar after the overnight soak and keep it away from sunlight.

Every several hours, add water to the jar and drain the lentils again.

As this process continues, tiny white tails will appear in 1 to 2 days or up to 4 days, if you choose to sprout for a longer period of time.

Spread all the sprouted lentils onto a paper towel on a baking sheet and let dry.

Store in a secure container in the refrigerator.

Enjoy lentils for a afternoon snack or add to your favorite salad or cold dish.

Mung Bean is another bean that is offered in a variety of cuisines, particularly Chinese cuisines.

It takes about 2-5 days to sprout Mung and lasts up to 2-6 weeks in the refrigerator after sprouting is completed. This beans offers an array of vitamins and minerals, including Vitamins A, B, C and E; magnesium; an excellent source of protein; iron, calcium and potassium, which will be efficiency used by the body after sprouting.

All you need:

Mung Beans, 2/3 c.

Mason Jar, 1 quart or a Kitchen Seed Sprouter

Water, 2 c.

Cheesecloth, 3-4

All you do:

- Simply wash beans in cold water then drain.

- Add beans to a mason jar and fill water 2-3 times as much as the Mung beans.

- Soak for at least 8 hours or overnight.

- Drain the water and add fresh cold water again, repeat the process.

- To drain, use cheesecloth or a paper towel and keep the lid covered with a light cloth.

- Avoid sunlight and keep stored at room temperature.

- Within 2-3 days, you will see little roots formed. The longer you sprout, the longer the roots will be.

Some examples of seeds that are suitable for sprouting:

Mung beans, lentils, chickpea, pea, sesame, sunflower, alfalfa, adzuki beans, Pumpkin Seeds, hazelnut (soaking), radish seeds, flaxseeds and more.

For more information about sprouting I highly recommend Ann Wigmore's book:

The Sprouting Book: How to Grow and Use Sprouts to Maximize Your Health and Vitality

CHAPTER 3

GETTING DEEP INTO YOUR MUSCLE

The first thing I want us to do is determine which type of muscles you have. There are two major classes of muscle:

Sarcoplasmic Hypertrophy – as the name suggests, these are muscles made when the sarcoplasm (fluid) levels are increased. This is as a result of training with minimal weight for many reps and very short intervals. Your muscles will puff up alright, but you will still not be strong enough to lift heavy weights. This type of muscles is very common with beginners.

Myofibrillar Hypertrophy – these are the fibrous type of muscles that we all look to have. The myofibrils are components of the muscle cell. With this type of muscle, you are going to be strong enough to lift very heavy weight without straining yourself too much. The best technique to use in order to attain these muscles is to train on heavy weights for short reps of 8-10 with a rest time of about 2 minutes.

It is now time for us to dissect the myofibrillar hypertrophy as this is what we as bodybuilders are interested in.

The three muscle fibers

I want to give you a little homework, the next time you go to the gym, pay close attention to the people there in terms of how big they are and find out how long it has taken them to get where they are. We are all built differently and have different classes of fibers. There are three muscle fibers and we are going to look at each of them but I want you to pay more attention to the third type if you are out to gain mass and muscle.

Slow-twitch muscle fibers

You probably know of someone who has been going to the gym for a number of years now but still has very tiny muscles even though he can lift weight for long intervals without getting weak. This is because this person is working mostly on the slow twitch fibers that allow him to train for long without tiring. This person would make an amazing marathoner but as is evident, not a very good bodybuilder. These muscles are essentially made for aerobic activities.

Fast-twitch muscles

There is a class of men/ladies in the gym who everyone wants to be like. You know what I am talking about. They always walk into the gym with confidence with their ripped muscles and lift weight so effortlessly. This is because these individuals are working mostly on the fast twitch muscles, which are great for anaerobic activities, with the techniques we'll mention soon. These people would make the worst marathoners in the world, but they will sure become excellent bodybuilders.

Hybrid muscle fibers

Now imagine a combination of type 1 and type 2 muscle fibers! This is what any bodybuilder worth his/her salt should be aiming for. These are super muscles that are built for both aerobic and anaerobic activities. With these muscles, you are going to have unmatched strength and endurance thanks to the greater mitochondrial concentration that translates to more energy for your muscles.

By applying certain scientific principles, it is possible to create hybrid super muscles that have the best characteristics of both Type I and Type II muscle fibers.

To create these 'hybrid super muscles' we are reconfiguring Type I and Type II muscle fibers into a new variety of muscle fiber (Type III) that has endurance, strength and greater mitochondrial density. The greater the mitochondrial density, the more energy we have available for our muscles.

Mitochondria are essentially the muscle cells' powerhouses, taking nutrients, breaking them down and producing energy for the muscle cells. The form of energy used to power our cells is known as adenosine triphosphate (ATP).

When you increase the mitochondrial density of muscle fibers, you boost mitochondrial capacity to burn fat for conversion into ATP. This enhanced utilization of fat for energy brings about a process known as 'muscle shifting,' which results in stronger muscles, increased lean muscle mass and a decrease in body fat.

INCREASED MITOCHONDRIA = INCREASED ATP.

The result is a great muscle shift to very strong muscles that are clearly defined and very low in body fat.

The process of creating these super muscle fibers involves reinforcing the type 2 muscle fibers to have endurance.

We are going to use one strategy to attain these super muscles:

Kill two birds with one stone

If you ask many trainers and instructors about bodybuilding the first thing they will tell you is that you cannot gain bulk and definition at the same time. Well, I would like to introduce a new school of thought; first look at this ol'skool method of bodybuilding before I give my two-cents on this topic.

In the massing phase, you eat a lot of calories and work out like a gladiator with the aim of getting hulk-big. In the process, you can't avoid packing fat alongside muscle so you will have to shed off the extra fat in order to get muscle definition.

When you are cutting on fat, you have to reduce the amount of calories you take every day and also do more of cardio.

The main reason why I disagree with this method is that you are putting your body under too much stress;

first we are eating a lot, next we are eating little...you are confusing your body.

You should approach bodybuilding as 'killing two birds with one stone.' That is gain mass and muscle definition at the same time. Our super muscles utilize the highest percentage of body fat compared to any other type of muscle fiber thus you are going to be getting bigger and more defined. This is very possible with the right training and a raw vegan diet. We are going to use vamped-up training techniques (in chapter 4) that are going to leave all your gym buddies asking you for the secret to your strong, ripped body!

Muscle Mechanics and Precise Training Targeting Guide

Increased <u>Loop-back</u> Training System®

You will now be presented with a detailed explanation for each separate muscle group and the way to target and train a particular muscle.

You will be taught the mechanics behind every exercise and its influence on a specific muscle or a group. This will enable you to organize your workouts in a way that provides the optimum muscle growth and strength increase in a shortest possible period of time.

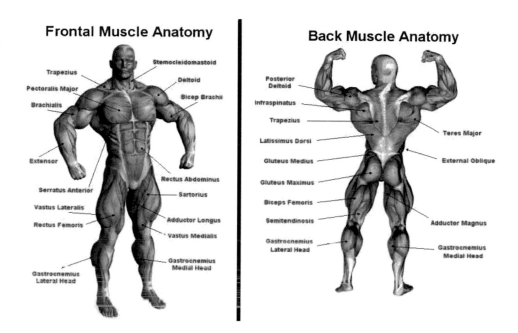

Frontal Muscle Anatomy

- Trapezius
- Sternocleidomastoid
- Deltoid
- Pectoralis Major
- Bicep Brachii
- Brachialis
- Extensor
- Serratus Anterior
- Rectus Abdominus
- Sartorius
- Vastus Lateralis
- Rectus Femoris
- Adductor Longus
- Vastus Medialis
- Gastrocnemius Medial Head
- Gastrocnemius Lateral Head

Back Muscle Anatomy

- Posterior Deltoid
- Infraspinatus
- Trapezius
- Teres Major
- Latissimus Dorsi
- Gluteus Medius
- External Oblique
- Gluteus Maximus
- Biceps Femoris
- Semitendinosis
- Adductor Magnus
- Gastrocnemius Lateral Head
- Gastrocnemius Medial Head

As you can see from the graphic, your body consists of couple of major muscle groups and we will apply the best bodybuilding practice in a process of segmentation. Your daily training session will look like this:

GROUP 1 - Chest, Triceps, Calves
GROUP 2 - Back, Biceps, Abs
GROUP 3 - Shoulders, Traps, (Calves)
GROUP 4 - Legs, Forearms, (Abs)

<u>Group equals your single training session.</u>

As you could see, Calves and Abs are repeated twice within one training week. This is the most effective segmentation of the muscle groups as you won't overload one particular and decrease the maximum output.

For instance, if you train Chest and Shoulders within a same session, you will exhaust your Shoulders while working Chest exercises.

Things to know before we start...

IMPORTANT: You will apply **Increased Loop-back System**® when executing every exercise as this is a proven method for achieving fast and effective muscle and strength gains:

- *Week 1 and 2* - low weights; 4 sets; 12 reps; rest-pause in last set

- *Week 3 and 4* - increase weights; 3 sets; 6-9 reps; drop-sets in last set

- *Week 5 and 6* - further increase weights; 3 sets; 6-8 reps; rest-pause in last set

- *Week 7 and 8* - maximum weight-overload; start with MaxPain® negative resistance concept at least once for each muscle; use spotter on bench press!

- Repeat the period by gradually increasing the overall weight for each following loop-back

- Apply 3/1 split system, where you train for 3 days and rest for 1 day.

ADDITIONAL NOTES:

The above presented loop-back training system is advised to be used for each particular exercise where you are using weights, during the entire workout program. Make sure to note your progress in maximum weight load used for each exercise, so you would know how much to add or deduct in each following cycle.

This simple, yet effective system yields unreal results in a matter of weeks.

When you are in your "rest day", do cardios and stretch your body. Push-ups and running or some sport are highly recommended. Make sure to avoid fast-digesting carbs.

Advice Pool

- Do a proper warm-up before each training session. You need to lubricate your joints and warm-up the muscle fibers in order to prevent injuries and to yield the best results.

- Control the position of your back in every exercise. It is extremely easy to hurt your back if your spine isn't in absolutely straight line all the time. Use wide belt and a spotter (training buddy.)

- Control your breathing as it is essential to oxygenate your blood system to peak your energy output. Just follow the rhythm of your body and you'll know exactly when to inhale and when to exhale.

- Remember having fast-digesting carbs in the middle of your training session. This is critical to grasp in order to make proper preparations prior to leaving for a gym.

What follows is a core of your future success in muscle growth and strength gain.

Let's start...

GROUP 1 - Chest, Triceps, Calves

Chest

Your chest consists of three separate, yet interconnected muscles:

- ***Pectoralis major - clavicular***, is the smaller, upper portion of your anterior chest muscle, connected with anterior deltoid muscle of your shoulders;

- ***Pectoralis major - sternal*** , is the bigger, lower portion of your anterior chest muscle, also connected with anterior deltoid;

- ***Pectoralis minor*** is positioned underneath the *pectoralis major*, stretching diagonally from the edges of your internal rib cage (where it is connected with ribs) to the lateral deltoid muscle.

Their main function is to move shoulders in 4 different actions allowing your upper arms to: move away from your body; move across; toward your chest and upwards (*i.e. throwing a ball or picking something from the ground, clapping your hands,*

Muscles of The Shoulder and Chest
Anterior View

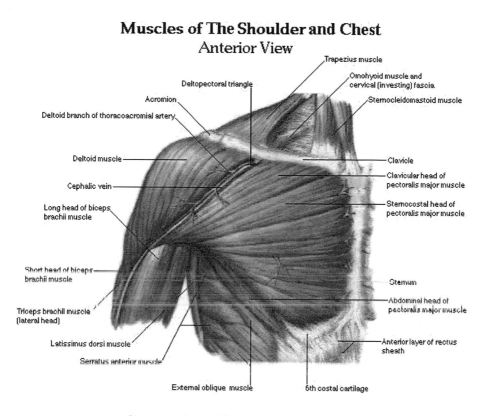

arm wrestling and making sure your arms are
attached to your body.)

From the perspective of bodybuilding, you will
target the lower part of pecs and the upper part of
them, by using a set of exercises.

EXERCISES:

Declined Bench Press - you will start with hitting
your lower pecs.

- Lie down on a declined bench and let your grip be outside the shoulder width (your torso is declined.)

- Push up from the chest until your arms are straightened; exhale during movement.

- Reverse the action and inhale.

Bench Press - this will hit the both upper and lower chest muscles. It's same as the Declined version, but you are lying entirely horizontally.

Incline Bench Press - this will hit the upper part of your pecs.

- With your back inclined by 45°, you are pushing barbell vertically from the perspective of the floor.

- Breathe out when pushing up, and breathe in when reversing the movement.

Dumbbell Butterfly Press - this will hit the interior part of your pecs, creating a distinct space between left and right chest muscle.

- Lie down on a bench. Spread your arms, with elbows under the horizontal line of your body and palms in line with your body. Your arms will not be straightened entirely, but under a small angle.

- Push up until one dumbbell touches the other in a same time, right above the center of your chest.

Make sure that you do not change the angle of your arms in any time.

High-pulley Cable Crossover - you are targeting your lower chest while eliminating contribution from your triceps.

- Pull the cables simultaneously by making a diagonal movement toward your pelvis.

- Hold it for a second and then slowly release the cables.

There is a certain advantage in doing pecs' exercises with nothing but dumbbells. In difference from classic barbell bench press, working with dumbbells makes exercise even harder as you need to employ additional force to achieve simultaneous movements of both arms.

Triceps

This is a relatively large muscle group at the back of your upper arm, consisting of three separated muscles: **long head, lateral head** and **medial head**. It is an extensor of an elbow and commonly employed when there is a need for a precise movement of the forearm as it will fixate both elbow and shoulder.

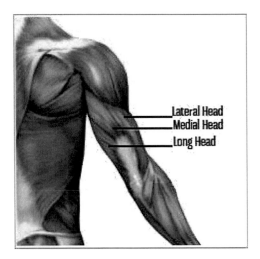

- *Lateral head* is in maximum use when there is a need for a short, high-intensity output of force.

- *Long head* is employed when there is a need for a sustainable and longer lasting generation of force or in cases where shoulder and/or elbow joints have to be fixated.

- *Medial head* is used at more precise movements with low-intensity force generation.

By knowing these primary kinetic facts of the triceps, we can now apply precise exercises to hit each of 3 muscles with an utmost precision, yielding superior results.

EXERCISES:

Dips - used as general warm-up this exercise will fire up all three major muscles within the triceps.

- You will use your own body weight to do this - 3 sets; 12-15 reps.

- Bend your knees slightly and put the bulk of the body weight directly on your triceps.

- Lower your body down until you reach close to 90°angle between upper arms and forearms.

- Then lift back up. Make sure that the forearms are straight so you would use nothing but the triceps to execute this exercise.

Band Scull Crusher - this exercise will hit the long head and medial head of the triceps mostly.

- Lie down and grab the band, placing it right above your forehead.

- You upper arm is vertical to the floor and you are pushing up by extending in the elbow until your arms are straight.

Triceps Pressdowns - this will mainly hit the lateral head.

- Your forearm is parallel to the floor and a bit inside the shoulder width, while your elbows are on your torso. *Remember: closer the grip; more precise isolation of the triceps exists!*

- Press down slowly, exhaling in a same time. Inhale and slowly reverse the movement of your forearms until reaching the starting position.

Reverse Grip Cable Pushdowns - this is a highly isolating exercise and in a single hand execution version, you are able to target nothing but the three muscles of triceps.

- Grab the bar of a high pulley machine in your shoulders width.

- Press down and slowly reverse the movement until you reach close to 90° between your forearm and upper arm.

Calves

This is a group of muscles reaching from your knee down to your foot. They are responsible and essential for movements of the feet (walking and running), and flexing the knees.

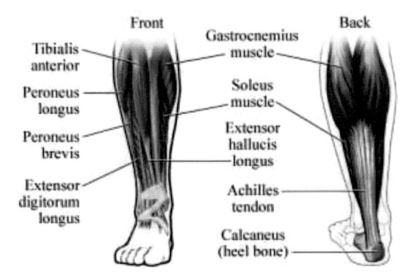

Calves consist of anterior and posterior group of muscles, all attached to both knees and feet. While you'll develop each of them, your focus will be on 2 posterior and 1 anterior muscles.

Posterior muscles, also known as *triceps surae* (3-headed calf muscle) are situated at the back of your lower leg. As plantar flexors they are responsible for the movement of your foot where the angle between sole and back of the leg will decrease (i.e. pressing a car pedal, ballerina on her toes):

- *Gastrocnemius* - a large 2-headed muscle (lateral or inner head; medial or outer head), situated at the upper portion of the back of your lower leg. When fully developed two heads will form the upside-down heart shape. In addition, this muscle is a knee flexor.

- *Soleus* - is situated under the gastrocnemius, and only the outer parts of it are visible, but when fully developed it gives a width to calf. In difference from gastrocnemius, soleus reaches all the way down to the foot.

Anterior muscles are extensors responsible for dorsi-flexion and inversion (movement of the foot towards inside like in a case of a twisted ankle) of your feet.

- *Tibialis anterior* - positioned at the front (anterior) side of your calves, this muscle is an extensor. It dorsal flexes your foot in non-weight-bearing leg (lifts medial edge of the foot like when you walk uphill), while in a weight-bearing foot it pulls the leg closer to foot.

EXERCISES:

Standing Calf Raise - targets gastrocnemius and depending of the angle of your feet (tilted inwards or outwards), you will hit lateral or medial head more.

If possible, use the machine and make sure that your back are straightened!; otherwise you are risking a lower back injury.

[NOTE: if you are suffering from that kind of injury, avoid this exercise and try calf press instead (will yield lower results.)]

- Elevate the front part of your feet by 2 inches (put something hard and fixed underneath) if you are doing this exercise with barbells.

- Push up concentrating on calves to execute the movement.

- Stop for a second and slowly reverse the movement until your feet are under the standing line and your calves are fully extended.

Donkey Calf Raise - hits gastrocnemius and it is superior to Standing Calf Raise because the bent-over position isolates gastrocnemius more effectively.

- Place your forearms on a high bench (in line with your hips) and let your spotter climb on your lower back, or use the machine.

- Incline the front of your foot by two inches and push up fully concentrating on the movement; hence your gastrocnemius muscles.

<u>Seated Calf Raise</u> - this will hit soleus, but will also employ the anterior muscles of calves.

- Make sure to elevate the front part of your feet by 2 inches before starting this exercise. This will yield maximum result as your calves will be fully extended.

<u>To target *tibialis anterior*</u>, elevate your heel by 2 inches by placing a fixed plate underneath. Place dumbbell on a phalanxes of your toes and lift it by inclining your foot. Concentrate on movement.

GROUP 2 - Back, Biceps, Abs

Back

This is the largest group of muscles on your entire body and we will break them into 3 separate groups: **Lats** (*latissimus dorsi*), **Rhomboids** and **Lower Back**. That way we are able to apply a specific exercise to target each group.

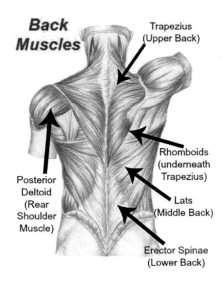

Back Muscles

Trapezius (Upper Back)

Rhomboids (underneath Trapezius)

Posterior Deltoid (Rear Shoulder Muscle)

Lats (Middle Back)

Erector Spinae (Lower Back)

[NOTE: Traps (trapezius) make a large part of the back muscles and from the perspective of bodybuilding (in difference from the usual anatomy); they fall into a group along with shoulders (deltoids.)]

Back muscles provide a main support for your body (head and torso), with upper portion of muscles (including traps) in a role of major structural support for head with limited movement ability. This is due to the fact that each rib is connected with the muscular tissue of the upper portion.

Lower back on the other hand, provides more room for movement (back and forward bending).

Latissimus dorsi (*eng.-broadest muscle of the back*) - is the extensor and adductor of your torso, while in conjunction with *teres major* it helps reversing the humus (upper arm bone) from elevated position. In addition, this large muscle is responsible for flexion from extended position and inner rotation of shoulder joint.

Rhomboids - Consisting of *rhomboid major* and *rhomboid minor*, these muscles are situated beneath trapezius muscle. *Major* is responsible for holding the scapula, but when employed with *minor*, when trapezius is contracted, they retract the scapula.

Lower back (*erector spinae*) - long muscles (group of several muscles) forming a bulk between first sacral and first lumbar vertebra, from where separate "branches" are stretching all the way up connecting with 7th rib on the outer side and first thoracic vertebra of the spine. Their main function is extension of vertebral column (side-to-side, straightening of the back, antagonistic movements of head and chest.)

Take a really good care of your back when training. If you allow damage or force injury of your back, the quality of your life will deteriorate. If you are a young man or woman, acute injury caused by the forced trauma will reflect as a chronic ailment and possible disability in a later stage of your life.

EXERCISES:

<u>Wide Grip Pulldown</u> - you are hitting *rhomboids, lower parts of traps* and also *latissimus dorsi.*

- Pull the bar on your chest and slowly extend all the way up. Breathe in while extending; breathe out while pulling.

<u>One-Arm Dumbbell Row</u> - this will target both *lats* and *rhomboids*.

- One knee on the bench with dumbbell in opposite arm. Your other hand serves as a major support and control the straight alignment of your back.

- Pull up by flexing in the elbow until your upper arm is parallel to the floor.

- Look straight forward! This will further ensure the correct alignment of your back.

<u>Standing Pulldown</u> - you are targeting *lats* directly.

- Lean backwards (entire vertical line of your body) and use one of your legs for additional support by pushing against the machine.

- Pull the bar all the way and reverse slowly, exhaling.

- Switch supporting legs

There is a variation of this exercise where you are sitting and leaning all the way back, mimicking the barbell rows.

<u>Bent-Over Barbell Rows</u> - ultimate exercise for *latissimus dorsi* but has to be executed with caution because of extremely high risk for potential back injury. It is advised to execute this exercise with spotter who will apply pressure on your lower back. Not for beginners!

- Bend over and hold a wide grip. Look straight ahead.

- Pull up the barbell to your lower abs. If you pull it more to your chest you will be targeting your rear deltoid.

In addition, this exercise impacts rear deltoids and biceps to some extent.

Seated Cable Rows - this hits the *lower back* muscles (*erector spinae*) along with medium impact on *latissimus dorsi*.

- Straighten your back and pull the cable to your upper abdominal region.

- Hold the cable for a second and then slowly reverse the movement.

Barbell Deadlifts - will hit the *lower back* in extreme manner.

- Your grip is wide and barbell is in front of you.

- Pull up only with your back and reverse the move, going down until your thighs are parallel with the floor (you will crouch so your legs will be employed in this exercise - try to diminish the role of your legs).

Biceps

The most distinct part of your body and one most likely to be "presented" to others are your biceps. As a kid you were probably showing off the bulge under

your sweatshirt ☺

Did you know that Arnold Schwarzenegger originally trained only his biceps and became a local biceps champion! Only later he started to work on other parts of his body. In his mind, only a gigantic biceps counted.

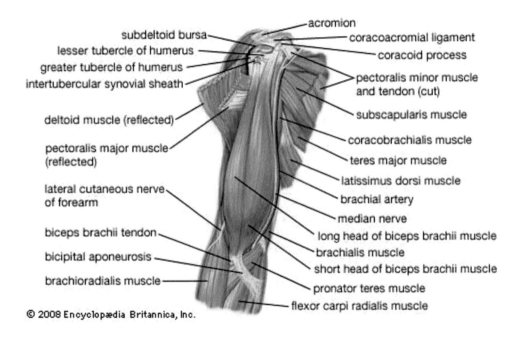

© 2008 Encyclopædia Britannica, Inc.

Biceps brachii or commonly known as **biceps** are in fact 2 muscles (exterior-*long head*; interior-*short head*), starting at scapula, forming a single muscle body at the middle of the upper arms, ending at the elbow joint.

Biceps work across 3 joints with main functions to supinate forearm and flex the elbow. Both of *biceps brachii* muscles are largely supported by *brachialis* muscle - a most powerful muscle in function of flexing the forearm.

Brachialis, located beneath the *brachii*, is attached to the lower arm differently, allowing it to generate more force than *brachii* in action where you are flexing your forearm in elbow joint.

Biceps is mostly employed when the forearm is supinated (palms are facing up), and this is the reason why you will hit it mostly with biceps curl exercise. In fact, *brachii* is best employed when you are supinating your forearm, turning your palm upwards, while your arm is least slightly flexed in elbow joint.

Take a dumbbell, flex your arm a bit in elbow and start turning your palm upwards and backwards - you will feel the pressure on both long and short head of your biceps.

In situation where your forearm is in pronation (palms are facing down), one other muscle will be maximally employed: *brachioradialis* muscle.

Brachioradialis is a powerful flexor of the elbow joint, helping *brachii*. But, when your forearm is in the middle point between supination and pronation in both radioulnar joints (elbow being one, and wrist being the other), *brachii* is in disadvantage due to its position and main action is performed by *brachioradialis*.

In practice, this means that if you want to specifically target the *brachioradialis* muscle, you will rotate your lower arm by 45° inwards (from a hammer holding position) and perform a *curl* by flexing in your elbow and pulling slightly upwards to your chest, maintaining that 45° angle at all times.

You start by isolating the biceps in elbow flexion. To do that you will place your shoulders in hyperextension (simply straighten your back and push your shoulders backwards.)

- To target the _long head_ and _brachioradialis_ muscles when using dumbbells, let your palms face each other. If you are using barbell, grip must be inside the shoulder width.

- To target _short head_ with dumbbells, palms are facing up. When exercising with barbell, your grip will be outside the shoulder width.

Another approach when exercising with barbell is to pull your elbow behind your back to target the long head, or push them forward, in front of your vertical line, to hit the short head.

EXCERICES:

Alternate Incline Dumbbell Curl - Only forearms moves and your elbows are close to your torso. You are targeting _biceps brachii_ and _brachioradialis._

- As you pull the dumbbell, rotate your wrist if you are targeting short head.

- When the dumbbell is in line with shoulder, hold it for a second and slowly bring the dumbbell back; one hand at the time.

Barbell Curl - Stand up straight and decide whether you are targeting the long head or short head, meaning that your grip will be outside the shoulder line or inside it.

Reverse Barbell Curl - you will target *brachioradialis* muscle.

- With overhand grip in shoulder width, flex in elbow and avoid movements of upper arms until reaching the end position where your elbows will move forward a bit.

Preacher Curl - You are targeting *short head* mostly but as your palms are slightly tilted inwards due to the shape of an EZ bar, you will impact the *long head* and *brachialis* also. The important part of this exercise is to contract your biceps to the max when you reach your shoulder line and to hold that position for a second.

Use the overhand grip in preacher curl to hit *brachioradialis* muscle.

Cable Hammer Curl - this targets *brachioradialis*. Execute exercise same as you would with classic Biceps Cable Pull but let your palms face each other (like holding a hammer.)

Dumbbell Concentration Curl - *long head* of *biceps brachii* and *brachialis* muscle.

- Sit on a bench and place back of your upper arm on your thigh.

- Fully extend your arm.

- Curl by flexing in your elbow. The critical thing is to concentrate on the movement and to execute it slowly.

Abs

The all-times 6-pax! Who don't want those, right?
But, your abdominal muscles are here for something
more important than showoffs. Having strong and big
abdominal muscles can make difference between life
and death.

Abdominal muscles, other than being a structural
support when combined with back muscles, assist
in breathing and can prevent a hyperextension.
Hyperextension is an abnormal increment of your
lungs.

In addition, your abdominal muscles safeguard
the vital organs, majority of which is situated right
underneath them.

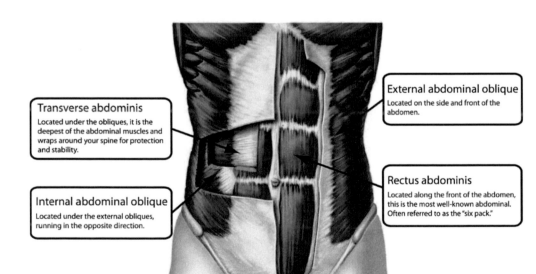

External abdominal oblique
Located on the side and front of the abdomen.

Transverse abdominis
Located under the obliques, it is the deepest of the abdominal muscles and wraps around your spine for protection and stability.

Rectus abdominis
Located along the front of the abdomen, this is the most well-known abdominal. Often referred to as the "six pack."

Internal abdominal oblique
Located under the external obliques, running in the opposite direction.

There are 3 layers of abdominal muscles: *transverse abdominis, internal abdominal oblique and external abdominal oblique.* They all merge with *rectus abdominis* in the center, shielding it.

Rectus abdominis is what you know as "6-pax". It's the outer layer consisting of parallel segments, reaching from the chest, down to pelvis. Main function is postural but it is also responsible for flexing the lumbar part of spine (crunching.)

External abdominal oblique is the largest and in the same time most superficial of all three lateral, anterior abdominal muscles. It pulls your chest downwards but also compresses the abdominal cavity.

Internal abdominal oblique is an intermediate muscle below external oblique with 2 main and important functions:

- It opposes the diaphragm reducing the volume of chest cavity while you are exhaling;

- By contracting, it side bends the torso, bringing chest closer to hip on the same side.

Transverse abdominals is the deepest muscle tissue on front and side of the abdominal wall, playing major role in stabilization and movements of the core (torso without limbs.) It does that by compressing ribs and organs inside the abdominal region. Core stability is therefore ensured as the thorax and pelvis are controlled (stable.)

EXERCISES:

Crunches- targeting the *middle portion* while impacting the upper one.

- Lie down, bend your knees and put your arms behind your head.

- Pull your torso up and slowly reverse the movement. As you progress through the program, increase the load by placing a 5-10 pounds plate on your chest and hold it with your arms crossed.

Oblique Crunches - you are targeting the *entire abdominal region including the sides.*

- Lie down and bend your knees.

- Simultaneously lift your legs and your torso, but place the arm under the back of your head so that your torso would move to the side (left or right.) You may do a series with your left arm where your torso will move to the right and then switch it to right arm, or you may exchange the hands in each lift.

Cross-Body Crunch - similar to oblique crunches, this exercise hits the *entire abdominal region.*

- Lie down and bend your knees while placing your arms behind your head.

- Simultaneously lift your right knee and twist your torso while lifting it in direction of the moving knee. Switch direction of your torso by lifting the left knee in a following lift.

GROUP 3 - Shoulders, Traps

Shoulders and Traps are largely connected, but when applying best practice of combining the smaller group with larger, this is a perfect combo.

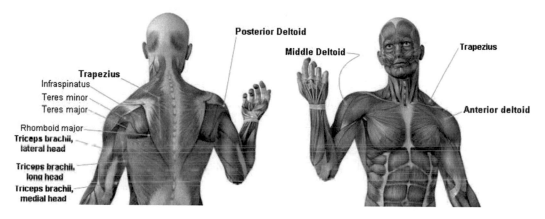

Shoulders (deltoids)

Your shoulder consists of 3 different muscles: **anterior** (front) deltoid, **lateral** (middle) deltoid and **posterior** (back) deltoid muscle.

All 3 are employed in shoulder abduction (flexing your shoulder joint upwards above your head.)

Anterior deltoid is positioned at the front side with main function to abduct the shoulder joint when your shoulder is externally rotated. It also assists in internal rotation of *humerus* and helps *pectoralis major* and *latissimus dorsi* in shoulder horizontal adduction.

Lateral deltoid is situated in the middle of the shoulder and it is most effective in lateral (along the vertical side line of the body) raise. Another important role of the lateral fibers is a precise and fast lateral abduction movement of the shoulder joint.

Posterior deltoid is positioned at the back side of your shoulder and it is most effective in transverse abduction of the shoulder joint - rear lateral raise. It is also a primary hyperextensor of the shoulder. It will be employed in rowing movements.

EXERCISES:

Side Lateral Dumbbell Raise - as it's been explained, change the alignment of your arms in relation to the vertical line of your body to hit *anterior or lateral deltoid*.

Seated Bent-Over Rear Delt Dumbbell Raise - this exercise targets the *posterior deltoid*.

- Sit on the bench and tilt your torso close to your knees.

- Raise the dumbbells and slightly bent your elbows inwards. Extend to the back as much as possible.

Front Dumbbell Raise - this targets the *anterior deltoid*.

- One hand at the time with palms facing down, raise the dumbbell all the way up, in line with your head. Elbows are slightly bent inwards to achieve the best targeting on the *anterior deltoid*.

Arnold Dumbbell Press - also known as a rotating shoulder press and was originally invented by the man famous for the size of his arms; 6 times Mr. Olympia - Arnold Schwarzenegger. You will push your deltoids to the limits and many argue that this is a *single most effective exercise for deltoids*.

- Sit on bench and hold dumbbells in line with your chest. Palms are facing you. As you lift, you are rotating your wrists by 180°. Push all the way up.

Upright Barbell Row you are targeting *anterior* and *lateral deltoids* with this exercise.

- Your grip is inside the shoulders width. Pull the barbell up to your chin and slowly reverse the movement.

Traps

Trapezius muscles are connectors of your back muscles and deltoids, responsible for rotating, retracting, elevating and depressing the scapulae. It moves scapula when spinal origins are stable, and moves spine when scapula is stabilized.

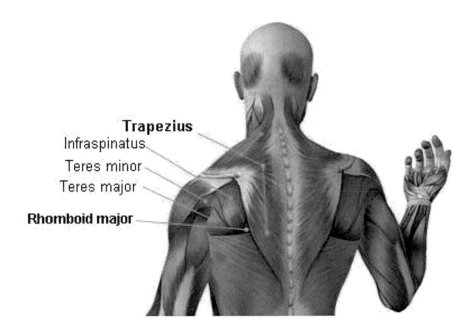

Trapezius
Infraspinatus
Teres minor
Teres major
Rhomboid major

We distinct 3 portions of *trapezius* muscle: **superior, middle** and **inferior**, based on the muscular connectors and directions of the muscular fibers. This segmentation is critical as you will have to adjust your exercises to target each of these 3.

Superior part of trapezius muscle is stretching from the back of your head and ends in line with your clavicles. Along with *inferior* it participates in rotation of scapula. It plays a major role in extending the neck when scapulae are stabilized.

Middle part is a narrow stretch of fibers, under *superior* part responsible for retracting the scapula.

Inferior part goes all the way down to the center of the back, covering *rhomboids* and connecting with *latissimus dorsi*.

While the most exercises you will do for your back muscles will also impact your traps, you need to target this large muscle separately. In addition, whenever you are working on your rear (posterior) deltoid; you are impacting the upper portion of your traps.

The importance of balanced development of all three portions of trapezius is not only aesthetic. Imbalance will seriously impact your overall posture.

EXERCISE:

Dumbbell Shrug - you are targeting the *superior* portion. It requires a high level of concentration because it is easy to cheat unconsciously.

- Your arms are straightened and in line with your vertical line.

- Shrug by focusing on your traps. The best approach is to close your eyes and make a mental image of the action.

Hang Clean - also targets the *superior*.

- Take the barbell with overhand grip, outside the shoulder width and incline your back slightly forward.

- Pull with your shoulders and start flexing in your elbow as you are lifting until you reach your chest line. Bend your knees a bit as you are progressing with the movement.

<u>Dumbbell Horizontal Extension</u> - targets the *middle* portion.

- Your starting position is similar to that in classic dumbbell shrug, but you will perform a horizontal action with your shoulders by hyperextending them backwards as much as you can.

To target the *inferior* portion, you'll execute an exercise, similar to Dumbbell Shrug, but instead of shrugging, you will force your shoulders down by keeping a straight, vertical line of your entire body.

GROUP 4 - Legs, Forearms

Legs

Consisting of the front and back muscle groups, the function of the upper legs muscles is the movement of your hip and flexion of your knee. In conjunction with calves, these muscles will lift you up from a seated position.

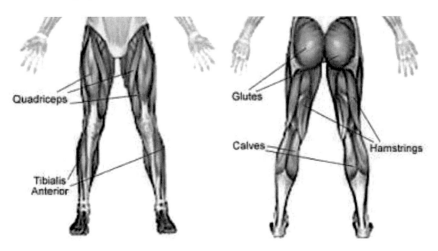

The <u>anterior</u> (frontal) side of your leg is dominated by the large muscle group known as **Quadriceps** *(quadriceps femoris)*. *Quadriceps* consists of four muscles: *rectus femoris, vastus intermedius, vastus medials* and *vastus lateralis.*

While quadriceps is primarily knee extensor, *rectus femoris* participates in flexing of hip joint.

On <u>posterior</u> (back) side we distinct:

- **Gluteus maximus** (<u>glutes</u>) are 2 large muscle groups above the femurs, at the back of your pelvis. They are extensors and lateral rotators of your hip joints, activated mostly when you are climbing the stairs or rising from seated to standing position. Two additional (lateral) parts of this muscle group are responsible for abduction and adduction of the hip. In addition, there are two even deeper muscles: *gluteus medius* and *gluteus minimus.* Their anterior fibers are rotating and flexing the hip while the posterior fibers act as a lateral rotators and extensors. When entire muscle is in action it abducts the hip.

- **Hamstrings** which are in fact four different muscles: *biceps femoris, semitendiosus, semimembranosus* and one below the knee joint- *popliteus.* Hamstrings are responsible for lateral and medial rotation of the knee joint, but also they are the flexors of the knee joint and extensors of hip joint.

EXERCISES:

Barbell Full Squat - you will hit the *glutes* and *quadriceps* <u>ONLY</u> if you squat below the knee line. If you have a bad knee, this exercise is not advised for you. Same is applied if you are suffering from acute or chronic back pains.

- Rest the barbell on your traps and shoulders.

- Make a full squat, going all the way down below the knee line and push back all the way up.

Barbell Deadlift - in difference from the version for your back, to really hit the *hamstrings*, you will incline the front of your feet by 2 inches.

Barbell Step Ups - targeting the *quadriceps*.

- Rest barbell on your shoulders and traps.

- Step up on a low platform (10 inches).

Barbell Hack Squat - hitting the *quadriceps* mainly but also impacts *hamstrings*, *calves* and *forearms*.

- In standing position, rest barbell behind your back, with your arms fully extended.

- Squat until your thighs are parallel to the floor.

One-Leg Barbell Squat - also known as a Bulgarian split squat, this will fire up your *quadriceps*. It's basically same as a Barbell Squat but with one leg lifted and pushed backwards. This exercise demands good balance and great experience.

<u>Lying Leg Curls</u>- exercise designed to isolate *hamstrings*. The best results are achieved on angled leg curl machines.

- Make the full movement, flexing in your knee. Pad of the machine's lever is on the upper portion of your Achilles tendon.

<u>Hip Thrusts</u>- targeting the *glutes*. It's important to focus on glutes whenever you are doing exercises that target them and to really squeeze them while executing the movement. This goes for every glutes-related exercise.

- Support your elbows with the bench and band your knees. Your ass is not touching the floor.

- Move your hip all the way up and hold it for a second.

- Slowly reverse the movement.

<u>Glute Bridge</u> - name says it all ☺

- Lie down and bend your knees, pulling your feet close to your glutes.

- Pull up from hips as high as you can and reverse slowly.

<u>One-leg Hip Thrusts</u> - targets your *glutes*.

- Lie down and place one foot on low (10 inches) bench.

- Fully extend your other leg and incline it little above the bench. This is your starting position.

- Push up from your hips as high as you can. Reverse the movement.

- Change the legs and repeat.

Forearms

Many will argue that there is no need for additional training of the forearms. I respectfully disagree.

Forearms play a major role in any exercise that is executed using your arms.

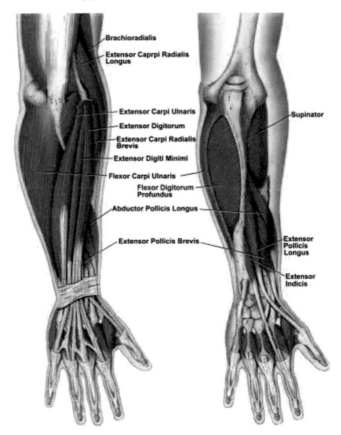

There are 4 groups of muscles in forearm segmented on account their main function: *extensors*, *supinators*, *flexors* and *abductors*, positioned on the inside and outside of your forearm (as you can see on graphic), reaching from the elbow joint all the way to the tip of your fingers.

Main functions of those muscles are:

- Rotation of your forearm in elbow joint;

- Every movement of your wrist, including twisting;

- Movements of your fingers.

There are two simple exercises that will enhance the muscle growth and overall strength of the forearms, making it that much easier for you to push your trainings beyond limits.

Dumbbell Wrist Curl - This exercise is designed to target the *inside section* of muscle group at forearm.

- Place your forearm on a bench but leave the wrist outside the bench, just enough to avoid blockage of the movement. In this exercise only your wrist is moving. Back of your palm is facing the floor.

- By using only your wrist and muscles of the forearm, pull the dumbbell up and then reverse the movement all the way down.

Apply the same as described above but this time back of your palm is facing up. You will hit the outside portion of the muscles of the forearms.

You don't have to do forearms exercises often. 2-3 times per month is an adequate frequency.

Now you have a detailed workout program with detailed insights of every muscle, its function and highly precise exercise to hit it and ensure its rapid growth.

But, there are some more aspects you need to comprehend in order to achieve superior results. Please read on.

CHAPTER 4

THE BEST TRAINING METHODS AND TECHNIQUES UNVEILED!

The greatest disservice you could ever do to yourself as a bodybuilder is to train hard without any goals in mind. Once you have identified exactly what you aim to achieve, now you can train smart. I have a great list of techniques that are going to transform your body in ways you didn't know were possible, on one condition though, you have to execute them near perfectly if not perfectly!

Compound vs. isolation exercises

- Compound exercises target more than one muscle group. Exercises involving pulling, pushing, squats and dead-lifts fall under compound exercises as they work on different muscles. For this reason, compound exercises are very effective and great for massing. However you need to carefully plan your workouts and maybe even enlist the help of a trainer or a training buddy. You will need to watch out and avoid overtraining a certain muscle that may have worked, using different exercises.

- Isolation exercises focus only on one muscle group at a time. For this reason, you will find yourself using smaller weights and having smaller growth. The main reason for this is a deficiency of stabilizer and synergist muscle development. If your stabilizer and synergist muscles are not strong enough, then your major muscles will never become big!

Compound exercise are more superior as they stimulate the most muscle fibers as possible, allowing all muscle groups to grow strong and big as you can use heavy weights to train to failure. Compound exercises improve your core and cause all the stabilizers and synergists come into play. Those assist the main muscles to lift heavy weights.

Your aim when training should be to put as much stress as possible on these supporting muscles. You can do this by doing free weight exercises such as squats, dumbbell press and bench press. You will get fatigued faster and even perform fewer reps but you will get stronger and gain more muscle. Always use heavy weights (heavy to you and not anyone else), as they stimulate most of your muscle fibers and this translates to more muscle mass.

Anaerobic vs. aerobic exercises

-   Anaerobic exercises focus on the type 2 muscle fibers, fast twitch muscle fibers, and are all about how much weight you lift and the force you use to train. Anaerobic exercises are great for gaining muscle and are done in low reps of 8-10 due to the heavy weights used.

-   Aerobic exercises on the other hand focus on the type 1 muscle fibers, slow twitch muscle fibers. They involve light weights done in many reps and usually focus on increasing the heart rate. Aerobic exercises are mostly used to enhance cutting.

Progressive overload

This is one of the greatest ways of challenging your muscles. You do this by gradually increasing the weights you use during weight training and this will lead to well defined and lean muscles. The process of progressive overload will lead to mini tears on your muscles that will be repaired during recovery- that is why sleep is very important as this is when your muscles get repaired and grow. The continued process of muscle tears, repairs and growth leads to bigger and stronger muscles.

Here is an illustration of this process:

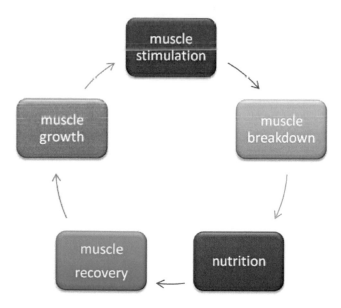

As you can see, the only way to have big, strong and defined muscles is to follow the sequence of muscle stimulation, breakdown, nutrition and recovery. This way your capacity to handle heavier weights will continue increasing progressively. Always remember that your muscles don't grow or cut when you are doing the actual workouts. In the contrary, your muscles grow during recovery when you get quality sleep and feed on a highly nutritious raw vegan diet.

On the other hand, failure to follow this sequence may lead to fatigue, muscle loss and eventual fat gain that can be very discouraging and have a negative impact on your self-esteem. You can easily get injured or cause some muscle problems.

The three phases of muscle growth:

-Stimulation

The best way to achieve this is through weight training. 20-50 minutes is all the time you need to stimulate your muscles.

-Recovery

This is a very important phase of muscle building as this is where muscle repair takes place. Having enough recovery time is going to guarantee you stronger muscles.

-Growth

The only way you can notice growth in your muscles is if you allow enough recovery time. Failure to do so will bring you to a standstill where no matter how much you train, you still don't see any noticeable change; that is what we call overtraining and can get to the point of muscle degeneration if not addressed soon enough!.

One week is enough time for these three phases to take place, just ensure that you give each phase the time and attention it deserves.

One-sided training

Muscle balance is very important in maintaining a good posture. Your right side should always be a mirror image of your left side and vice versa. One-sided training involves training one arm/leg at a time. This is very good for strengthening the weaker side.

You have to train smart when doing the one-sided exercises. For instance, I would advise you to add additional reps for the weaker limb. Say for example if you are doing 10 reps of dumbbell curls; and your right arm can comfortably do 10 reps of 25 pounds but your left arm can only do 6 reps; do the 6 reps with 25 pounds and then grab lighter weights and continue with the remaining reps (4). Always do this until your left hand is in a position to keep up with your right arm. Once you achieve this, you will notice an impressive ease in performing other exercises.

For maximum muscle gain, you should do around 3-4 exercises on each body part once or twice a week, depending on your level and let sleep and nutrition do the rest of the job for you.

Train to failure

Intensity

The first step in muscle building is to determine your intensity threshold. What do I mean by this? The ideal number of reps for intensive workouts is 8 -10 in 3-4 sets. If you can't get yourself to complete 8 reps then you know that the weight is too heavy for you and on the other hand if you are able to do more than 10 reps then the weight is too light for you.

Drop set

As the name implies, this technique involves weight training starting with a large weight then dropping the weight and going for more reps to the point of failure. This is one great way to train to failure as you are stimulating different muscle fibers. When you start with heavy weights, you are targeting a certain group of fibers, as you drop the weight; you go to a different group of fibers. This is a very effective technique that boosts high quality muscle growth due to the fact that you work on different muscle fibers all in one workout.

This is the best way to apply Drop-sets: you do your last set until reaching a full muscle failure. Then, you decrease the weights by 1-2 pounds and after 12 seconds push until failure. You then lose additional 1-2 pounds and reach the final muscle failure after max. 12 seconds break in between.

Rest-pause

Is applied in last set of a single exercise where you do rep without changing the weights until failure. Then, you wait max. 12 seconds and continue until reaching

another full muscle failure. Again, rest max.
12 seconds and reach the final muscle failure.

NOTE: Regularly practice both Rest-pause and Drop-sets by applying a "rotation principle", where you'll do Rest-pause for 1-2 weeks and then you'll switch to Drop-sets for 1-2 weeks.

Superset

If you want to have a short and sweet reminiscent time at the gym, supersets are the way to go. A superset involves bumping up your intensity in very short time duration. A superset involves doing an exercise and without resting proceeding to another one. Only after you are through with all the sets of each one of the exercises can you say you have completed 1 set of the superset. Rinse and repeat until you are through with all the sets of your superset.

Antagonistic supersetting is very effective when it comes to stimulating your muscles. This involves working on two opposite muscle groups concurrently for example; you can work on your chest and back; quads and hamstrings; biceps and triceps. Since you are stimulating opposite muscle groups, this allows you to lift more weight faster.

You can take supersetting a step higher by introducing giant sets. A giant set is similar to a superset, but you rotate between three or more workout stations as opposed to the two in supersetting. This is another great way to train opposing muscle groups and keep workouts intense.

Pyramid training

This is the perfect strength training workout as it utilizes both the upward and downward series in weight, sets and reps. You have probably used pyramids before only you didn't know what to call it.

Basically, pyramid training involves doing one or two exercises for a particular rep, say 10 and then working your way down to 1. The main intention of pyramid training is to fatigue your muscles and stimulate as many muscle fibers as possible thus maximizing muscle growth. Pyramids can be done as an upward or downward series in weight and reps. Upward pyramid allows you to warm up before going for training to failure with downward pyramid exercises.

Advanced techniques

Burnouts

A burnout set should be at the end of the body part workout, in order to completely fatigue the muscles. Burnouts combine pyramids and drop sets, working up to higher weights with low reps and then back down to lower weights and high reps(from 15 up to 100). This method encourages maximal glycogen depletion.
In order to avoid the risk of overtraining, make sure not to use burnout sets often.

MaxPain®

Is an extreme concept, used by the most successful bodybuilders and it is based on a negative resistance.

NOTE: There is a strong possibility that you will fall down on the ground after you finish with this type of exercise due to the extremely exhausting dynamics and muscle fibers overload.

You'll introduce this feature later in your program - in a point where you are fully prepared for it.

Basically, what you are going to do is to set your maximum weight for a specific exercise after a short warm-up. You will then reach a full muscle failure, take 10 seconds rest and do one more rep until next failure. In a next phase, you'll drop 2 pounds and repeat the above. Take 20 seconds break, drop additional 2 pounds and repeat the above. Follow this routine until you reach the minimum weight and make sure to achieve a full muscular failure at each rep.

What's important in this technique is: breathing! You need to breathe correctly to ensure proper oxidation of your body, critical for burning the energy.

Ultimately, MaxPain® can be used in conjunction with Supersets to yield superior gains. For instance, combine Barbell Curl with Triceps Pressdown and force your biceps and triceps to explode in size.

Diminishing set

With this technique you use a weight that limits you to 20 reps per set. Your goal is to complete 70 reps in as few sets as possible (preferably in just 4 sets). It might sound simple, after all if you do 4 sets of 20 reps each, that's a total of 80 reps. But, you will not be completing 20 reps in every set. That's because with diminishing set training, you are only allowed 2 minutes of rest in between sets. After reaching muscle failure in the first set (the 20 reps), your muscles will be so fatigue that that 2 minutes rest period will not be enough for your muscles to recover at that rep range. You may end up only completing half that many reps at the second set. Each success of set will push muscle fatigue even further so the number of reps you will able to complete on each success of set will continue to fall as you go.

You will be lucky if you can complete those 70 reps in 6 or 7 sets in the first time you use this technique.

One key to diminishing set training is finding a weight that limits you to 20 reps on the first set. If you find a weight that limits you to 19 reps, you are good to go too, however, if you can't complete at least 19 reps on the first set then that means that the weight is too heavy for you. If you can complete more than 20 reps in the first set, the weight is too light.

The second key to this training technique is making sure that you go to muscle failure on each and every set. If you don't hit muscle failure, it will be way too easy to complete 70 reps in 4 sets.

The third key to this training technique is making sure that you keep rest periods to exactly 2 minutes. Any longer than that, won't be a challenge. Any shorter than 2 minutes, will make it too hard to complete.

Forced reps

A forced rep is when you reach a muscle failure during a set and you have a training partner or a personal trainer which assists you and push you into doing more reps than you normally couldn't do on your own. With this method, more muscle fibers are being fatigued. This will also stimulate more growth and muscle density.

Your training partner is there to help you to get past the sticking point of your set and allow you to complete more reps beyond your normal range.

There are exercises which forced reps can be done without an assistant. For example, with one arm triceps extension, the other arm can be used to assist the arm that is being trained.

You want to make sure that you do not use this method in every single exercise that you do, since with forced reps, we are shocking the muscles.

Cheat reps

This is a method in which the bodybuilder is "cheating" the body, so he could load and lift heavier weights. The cheating is performed by deliberate swinging that help the body to lift a weight higher.

The good thing about cheat reps is that it can be done without a training partner. However, cheating may increase the risk of injury, if not performed with safety, since it exposes the bodily structures to forces to which they are not accustomed.

Partial reps

The idea around this method is when the bodybuilder is unable to do full reps throughout the range of motion, then he is performing partial reps (a smaller range of motion), in order to achieve superior load on the muscle.

Super slow

Super slow repetitions are performed with lighter weights. Super slow sets usually take about 14 to 15 seconds to perform 4 to 6 repetitions.

This means that you will move through the contraction portion (concentric) for 10 of those seconds, and the remaining 4 to 5 seconds will consist of the relaxation movement (eccentric).

Performing these sets will help you increase the time under tension, meaning that your muscles will have a stress loaded upon them during the concentric portion of the exercise.

Your body is going to use a higher number of muscle fibers since total muscular recruitment has a direct relationship with time under tension, degree of range of motion and total weight lifted.

	Endurance	Hypertrophy	Strength	Power
Time Under Tension	-	4-12 sec	1-2 sec	1 sec or less
Intensity	50%	75%	85%-95%	100%
Reps	15+	6-12	1-3	1
Sets	1	2-3	3-5	4-8
Rest	-	60-90 sec	2-4 min	3-5 min
Example	Distance cycling	Shoulder Press	Deadlift	Sprint/ box jump

Endurance – mostly aerobic

Hypertrophy – The ability to build tissues, get bigger muscles

Strength – The ability to move and lift heavy.

Power – Explosive movement. The amount of work performed per unit of time. Ability to perform a powerful movement in minimal time

These additional techniques, incorporated within your overall workout program, are crucial if you are aiming for a fast muscle gains. They ensure that you constantly "shock" your brain and muscles, not allowing them to adapt to a regime.

Muscle fiber stimulating workouts

Weaker Body Parts First

My suggestion would be to train your weakest body part or the one you want to improve at the first day of the week and either train the body part by itself or group it with a strong body part. That's because you are usually mentally and physically fresh at the beginning of the week.

The order of training your muscle groups

Different muscles in the body are classified as large and small. Legs, back and chest are considered large while biceps, triceps, forearms and shoulders fall under the small category. (If you are working two small groups at the same workout, triceps and biceps for example, you will also need to start with the larger group which is, in this case, the triceps).

So if you are training 2 or more body parts in one workout, the order in which you train them can GREATLY affect your muscle growth potential in each body part. Start your training off with the bigger muscle group.

These smaller muscles provide assistance to the larger muscles during training which is why you should not exercise the smaller muscles first if both muscle groups are being training in the same workout (example: Back and Biceps workout).

If you train Biceps before Back, your smaller muscles will become fatigued and won't be able to support the heavy weights required by the back exercises later in your workout routine. By working the larger muscles first and then moving onto the smaller ones you avoid undue strain while increasing muscle mass, density and strength. Therefore, the most important muscles to train first in a workout would be the larger ones when you have the most amount of energy.

Some more advanced muscle builders will do two training sessions in one day. Training different muscle groups in the second session than in the first training session of the day will still allow muscles time to rest and recover but allow the muscle builder to add in additional training sessions.

So here is a conclusion of some simple rules you need to follow for muscle gain:

• Train each body part once a week (Training a body part 2-3 times a week for muscle growth is DEAD WRONG!)

• Choose 3-4 exercises per body part (No need for more exercises)

• Train in the 8-12 rep range

• Always use progressive overload

• Rest for 1.5-2 minutes between sets

• Train to failure

• Choose exercises to train all parts(all muscle fibers) of each body part

If you follow the raw vegan lifestyle and the above muscle building strategies, I 100% guarantee that you will see strength improvement each training session and you will begin to see new muscle development in just weeks.

Weekly routines examples:

1. Monday – Chest and Abs

   Tuesday – Quads and

   Calves Wednesday – Back

   Thursday – Shoulders and

   Abs Friday – Hams and

   Calves Saturday – Biceps and

   Triceps Sunday – Off

2. Monday – Hams and Calves

   Tuesday – Back and Abs

   Wednesday – Shoulders and Triceps

   Thursday – Off

   Friday – Quads and Calves

   Saturday – Chest

   Sunday – Biceps and Abs

Exercise Examples:

Back

Wide grip pull ups – 3-4 sets of 8-12 reps

Dumbbell Pullover – 3-4 sets of 8-12 reps

Lat pull-downs - 3-4 sets of 8-12 reps

Seated Row with dumbbells – 3 sets of maximum repetitions possible

Biceps

Alternate incline dumbbell curls – 3-4 sets of 8 – 12 reps

Drag curl – 3-4 sets of 8 – 12 reps

Cross body hammer curl – 3-4 sets of 8 – 12 reps

Calves

Smith machine calf raises – 3-4 sets of 8-12 reps

Barbell seated calf raise – 3-4 sets of 8-12 reps

Single-leg calf raise with a dumbbell – 3-4 sets of 12-15 reps

Chest

Flat bench press – 3-4 sets of 8 – 12 reps

Decline Push-ups – 3 -4 sets of 8 – 12 reps (or maximum repetitions possible)

Incline Dumbbells press – 3 -4 sets of 8 – 12 reps Pec deck– 3 -4 sets of 8 – 12 reps

Quads

Barbell Squat - 3-4 sets of 8-12 reps Seated

Leg Press – 3-4 sets of 8-12 reps Lunches –

3-4 sets of 8-12 reps(each side) Leg

Extensions – 3-4 sets of 8-12 reps

Hams

Barbell Hip Thrust – 3-4 sets of 8-10

reps Stiff Leg Dead Lift – 3-4 sets of 8-10

reps Sumo Squat – 3-4 sets of 8-12 reps

Lying Leg Curls – 3-4 sets of 8-12 reps

Abs

Cable Crunches – 3-4 sets of 12-15 reps

Reverse Crunches – 3-4 sets of 15-20 reps

Decline crunches – 3-4 sets of 10-15 reps

Shoulders

Arnold dumbbell press –3 -4 sets of 8 – 12 reps

Close Grip Barbell Shoulder Press– 3 -4 sets of 8 – 12 reps

 T-bar Rows – 3 – 4 sets of 8- 12 reps

External Arm Rotations (Cable) - 3 -4 sets of 8 – 12 reps

Triceps

Dips – 3 – 4 sets of 8- 12 reps

Band Skull Crusher – 3 – 4 sets of 8- 12 reps

Reverse Grip Cable Push Downs – 3 – 4 sets of 8- 12 reps

Keeping your body fat low

Many factors, including weight, age, gender and activity level, determine the amount of calories needed per day. The use of an online calculator can give you a rough estimate; however, you can determine how many estimated calories you burn daily and then add on average anywhere between 250 to 500 calories daily. You are going to gain fat if you consume more fuel than your body actually use. It is important to monitor your weight regularly (e.g., once per week at least) to ensure that the right amount of calories is being consumed to meet your weight and muscle building goals.

It is important that your extra calories are comprised of good calories, not junk calories. Including a sprouts, vegetables, fruits, nuts and seeds that will help support your health and wellness goals. Timing is also an important factor as going longer than 3-4 hours will offset your metabolism and possibly increase fat storage.

I also suggest you incorporate HIIT in your weekly schedule:

What is HIIT?

HIIT is the acronym for high-intensity interval training. In this conditioning to exercise, a person fully engages the body of a high degree exercise in a fast and elaborate exercise. The process then involves short and often dynamic recovery sessions.

HIIT is also referred to as HIIE, an acronym for high-intensity intermittent exercise. Its other name is sprint interval training (SIT). Like said earlier, HIIT is a heightened sort of interval exercise, a training scheme where interchanging periods of quick and acute anaerobic exercises are engaged with the body getting little time to recover.

HIIT sessions are tailored to a session of a time frame of between three to thirty minutes. HIIT is a most recent and prove way in burning of body fat. It is an intensive and alternative aerobic choice. When contrasted with traditional cardio systems, it takes the shortest time to finish.

HIIT the Best Cardio to Burn Fat

Besides a severe fat burn, this training causes an increased aerobic capacity. This means that an increase in the oxygen intake means an all round aerobic capacity which increases faster more than with a low intensity endurance exercise.

HIIT body conditioning induces hormone production while it minimizes the respiratory exchange ratio during the day. HIIT has also an advantage of increased lactate thresholds. In simple terms, this is the body's ability to handle a heightened lactic acid development. Improved insulin sensitivity means the muscles ability to absorb more glucose rather than it being absorbed into the fatty tissues. And finally we have what we call anabolic effect.

When the interval training is merged with an uptake of more calories than one can burn, an effect is created which is called anaerobic. It is an effect that helps a person build muscles. On the contrary, when a firm cardio is engaged for long sessions, fewer muscles are build and it is referred to as catabolic.

HIIT is a hybrid system between high intensity aerobic work and very high intensity component to provide a maximal fat burning effect. In HIIT, the metabolic rate is hyped up to last twenty four hours long after training has ended. In essence, the body adapts itself to the speed of the exercise while calories are conserved.

Once a person engages in this type of exercise, the heart rate goes up while at the same time, lots of fat is burnt within a short period of time. With time, the person exercising will have a better athletic capability and an all rounded body wellbeing. On the contrary, slow aerobic action provides low impact on the joints which in turns create an ideal environment for obesity. The fat is burning directly which is contrary to the idea of burning of the total calories. This low aerobic action can take long periods of time. But its only advantage is its use as a recovery tool for people who have suffered from intensive training methods.

Why is HIIT better than slow cardio?

Heart Rate and Energy Sources During Workouts

The heart's maximum heart rate that one can attain through exercise stress is known as HRmax. It is the highest heart-rate value achieved in an all-out effort of the point of exhaustion. It is influenced by age. It is measured through what is called cardiac stress tests.

A person exercises and his actions are noted by an electrocardiography (EKG).

To further record the exercise the, a treadmill's intensity levels are heightened either through speed or at other times its slope. The process continues and the changes in the heart are observed on the EKG. From the results, the person is ordered to end the session. The duration of the test take between 10 to 20 minutes.

Target Heart Rate (THR) is also called Training Heart Rate. It is a projected range of heart rates that is attained when a person engages in aerobic exercise. Its function is to help the heart and even the lungs to benefit after a workout. To calculate one's Target Heart Rate, there's a factor called intensity which is shown as a percentage. The can be calculated as a range of 65%-85% intensity. An example of someone with a HRmax of 180 (age 40, estimating Hyrax as 220 - age), 65% intensity, (220 - (age = 40)) × 0.65 → 117 bpm 85% intensity, (220 - (age = 40)) × 0.85 → 153 beats per minute (bpm).

In order to understand the myth of fat burning zone, you will need to understand how your body uses energy when training. During exercise, your body uses too main sources of energy: Glycogen and fat. Glycogen is stored mainly in the liver and in your muscles.

Now where did the myth come from? Well, it is true that at lower exercise intensities the body uses more fat than glycogen as his energy source. But that doesn't mean that now you can just sit all day and burn fat.

At 50% of your max heart rate, your body burns a ratio of 60% fat to 40% glycogen. At 75% of your max heart rate, the ratio is 35% to 65%, and at even higher intensities, the ratio is even lower.

So are you still wondering why would you want to work out at a higher intensity if you burn a lower percentage of fat?

The answer is in the calories. The overall number of calories burned in and after exercise is called energy expenditure.

It is the total energy a subject will use in his workout. In a workout, calories which are burned are denoted as O2. The table below shows how calories are burnt during your workout.

30 Minutes of Training	Fat Calories that Burned	Glycogen Calories that Burned	Total Calories that Burned
Low Intensity Grouping (50%)	140	100	220
High Intensity Grouping (75%)	160	280	420

From the above table, a high percentage of fat calories are burned when the exercise is high intensity in contrast to a low one even though the fat burn is low.

The Afterburn Effect

An intensive exercise breeds a high afterburn effect. A good example is a person who sprints in 30 seconds with 5 round will experience a great afterburn in relation to a subject who just trots within a period of 30 minutes.

HIIT increases EPOC (excess post-exercise oxygen consumption) which in time increases your metabolism. EPOC will burn more calories for up to 24 hours after you finish your workout. You won't have something like this from lower intensity exercise. That's why you want to make sure not to do HIIT every day. The preferably amount is 2-3 HIIT per week.

Here, the amount of oxygen used is directly proportional to heat expenditure. An oxygen debt is created. The Excess post-exercise oxygen consumption (EPOC) is used to aid in increasing oxygen assimilation which aids the body in getting rest and get accustomed to the exercise.

Examples of HIIT workouts:

Different experts have different points of view on HIIT workouts. But they agree that it is impossible to carry out HIIT exercises every day. On one hand experts say that doing it twice or thrice every week delivers the anticipated results. But the caveat is that it should be carried out according to the laid down procedures.

If you just started training and incorporating HIIT in your weekly training routine, you will want to do a work-rest ratio of 1:4 for about 12-15 minutes, in order to get your body used to this kind of intensity.

So that means that for every 15 seconds of work, you rest 60 seconds.

As you get used to this kind of training, you can bring the ratio up to 1:2, 1:1 and eventually 2:1, when your work phase is twice the amount of time that you rest.

As you progress, you will be able to increase the duration of the training to -17,20 and 25 minutes.

BEGINNERS: work/rest ratio – 1:4, 1:2. Total training time: 12-20 minutes

Advanced – work/rest ratio – 1:1, 2:1 , 3:1. Total training time: 20-30 minutes

Examples of HIIT exercises:

Rope jump, Burpees ,Squat jumps , mountain climbers, sprints, box jumps, planks, pushups, high knees, jumping jacks

You can also use some martial arts techniques:

Muay Thai roundhouse kicks as fast as you can.
Act as if you want to hit a challenger's thigh or imagine it is his midsection. Redo this process till you tire. You may not be fast at the beginning but with exercise, you can kick higher.

The more advanced and flexible you are, the higher you can kick. As soon as you kick, you get your leg back. Use your hips to propel the kick. Your hips should be the first thing to move then your legs will follow. Swing your arms downward to kick.

If you are using your right leg to kick, swing your right arm and return it back as soon as you kick. If you are kicking with your left leg, swing your left arm and back as soon as you kick. Keep the hand that is not swinging in front of your face. For those of you experienced in martial arts, this kick is a little bit different from karate or Tae Kwon Do round house kicks. With karate or Tae Kwon Do, your legs extend fully and kick with your foot.

You can also use a heavy punching bag. A mixed martial art (MMA) bag is good or a boxing one. For example, you can give this bag serious jabs for twenty seconds. Intersperse the jabs with kicks on the bag with a fast speed. Take twenty seconds of rest and repeat the process for twelve minutes of these sets.

Last important tips:

Hydration

Water intake is very, very, very important in muscle building. It flushes out waste from your body, ensures oxygen and essential nutrients are taken to your cells and is the perfect lubricant for your joints. In short, what I am saying is that water should be part and parcel of your training regimen. Let me give you a brief list of the benefits of taking water:

- Boosts your strength

- Improves overall muscle growth and development

- Increases focus and attention

- Reduces fatigue

- Shortens recovery time

Make it a habit to drink water before, during and after a workout for optimal results. Fruits and vegetables are another great way to stay hydrated. They have lots and lots of water content inside them thereby helping you to reach for high levels of liquids in your body as well. The bonus is the essential nutrients you get from them.

Remember, some liquids are dehydrates. The more dehydrates you drink during the day, the more water you need to drink to stay hydrated. Coffee, tea, soda, and carbonated energy drinks are just some examples of dehydrates. Try to keep these drinks to a minimum and remember to drink more water if you are drinking dehydrates on a daily basis.

Sometimes bodybuilders have a hard time getting enough water in on a daily basis. Many find if you start drinking water early in the day, hydrate throughout and after your training sessions will help you keep your water intake high. Once you fall behind in your daily water intake or get out of the habit of drinking water regularly, it is sometimes hard to get back on track.

Eat! Eat! Eat!

One of the biggest mistakes you could ever make as a bodybuilder is to cut down on the calories you take. Let me shed some light here; calories are the sole fuel for your muscles and this is what makes your muscles grow. The bigger your muscles become, the more calories you will be required to eat to boost growth even further!

Don't be afraid to gain weight, you are supposed to support your muscle growth and the body's stress right now. This doesn't mean you can eat 6000 calories because you will gain fat of course, since the body will not use all these calories. Again, I suggest using cronometer or any other calculator to see where you are standing with your calories intake and then take the necessary steps from here.

Diversify on what you eat so that you get a wide variety of nutrients that are going to be used to speed up recovery and to help you bulk faster. By diversify, I do not mean that you can go on a junk spree or animal products. Absolutely not! The raw vegan diet has exactly what you need!

Make sure you include leafy greens such as lettuce, spinach, kale and other leafy greens as they are very high in nutrients and proteins. This will give you all the energy you need and also provide you with quality nutrition to speed up recovery.

CHAPTER 5

IMPORTANCE OF BEAUTY SLEEP

Sleep is one of the 'building blocks' for our super muscles. Remember we have been engaging in extreme resistance training in order to grow big muscles and shed any extra fat. This whole process is extremely stressful for our bodies and training recovery is a must if you are to notice any positive changes!

Unfortunately, in today's day and age, sleep has become very elusive. Our schedules are busier than ever and sometimes we have to sacrifice sleep for other things. This is the biggest mistake you as a bodybuilder should do as all the positive changes you had started noticing on your muscles will all come to a grinding halt!

Your body should always be your first priority. Always think of your body first; if you want to reach your goals, you must make some sacrifices!

I want us to get to the very core of sleep so that you get to understand and appreciate its role in training recovery and muscle growth.

Going to the very beginning; sleep during the day is different from sleep at night. During sunrise, when light is just breaking out, your body increases the release of adrenaline and dopamine which are active hormones that immediately decrease all sleep inducing agents and this is what makes you very alert in the morning.

As sunset approaches, so does the body's release of melatonin and serotonin which are relaxing hormones. Adrenaline and dopamine slowly reduce allowing you to relax and get ready for bed.

Sleep is anabolic. What does this mean?

When you sleep, this is the time your body recovers from training, repairs any damaged tissue and grows new muscle tissue. All this is attributed to the fact that growth hormones are released during sleep thereby making sleep anabolic.

Special neurotransmitters that promote effective and safe bodybuilding are replenished when sleeping. Some of these neurotransmitters are adrenaline, dopamine, acetylcholine and noradrenalin. These special neurotransmitters are what give you focus, motivation, attention, energy and muscular contractions. During intensive training, these neurotransmitters are depleted and can only be replenished adequately during sleep.

As a bodybuilder, your health should always be at tip top shape. Sleep is very important when it comes to boosting your immunity, mental health and every biochemical process in your body. Sleep deprivation will lead to a compromised immunity leaving you susceptible to diseases and when this happens, you might as well forget about bodybuilding for some time.

Muscle wasting is another inevitable consequence of sleep deprivation as the body does not have time to recover. In the end, you are going to have increased body fat and at the same time leave you more susceptible to injury and overtraining. Injury will arise since you are not getting enough rest but you still want to train so carelessness and dropping weights may be unavoidable.

Your sleeping environment will be the deciding factor of whether you get quality sleep or not. Aim at making your room very, very quiet and as dark as night in order for you to get the best quality sleep and therefore promote recovery.

Another thing that you should do is establish a routine that you follow every day before you sleep such as reducing or eliminating any physical activity 2 hours before sleeping; avoiding large meals just before going to bed and going to bed at the same time every day.

As we draw to an end, I want to emphasize that it is absolutely possible to be a bodybuilder and gain muscle mass on the raw vegan diet! You can train the same and even have more energy and power! This is the healthiest diet in the world and the best gift you can give your body. Muscles are made in the gym! Recovery is made in the kitchen.

When you give your body the proper fuel, amazing things happen! You will see it on your body, skin, mental clarity, emotional balance, health and the list goes on.

Tips to easily transition to a raw vegan diet

The transition to a raw vegan diet may pose some challenges, as many of the foods people enjoy contain high saturated fat, sodium, sugars, etc. People are used to cook their food.

It is best to transition slowly, by reducing 1-2 unhealthy foods each day rather than eliminating everything at once. This may lessen the overwhelming diet change. In addition, since raw foods contain highly fibrous components from the fruits and vegetables, a slow transition to raw eating will be beneficial for gut health, reducing unpleasant gastrointestinal (GI) effects, such as bloating and gas. Increasing water intake during the transition will help with GI symptoms as well.

Another way to incorporate more raw foods in your diet is the "raw till 4/6". The "raw till 4" or "raw till 6" is basically a lifestyle where you eat unprocessed raw foods until 4pm or 6pm, depends on the version that you choose. After 4pm/6pm you can eat a cooked meal of your choice but make sure you choose a healthy option and don't exaggerate with the portions.

Remember, healthy food is a gift and a reward that your body deserves every day. Your body is your temple. It is not a trash can. Don't just throw in stuff. Treat it with respect. Think about it: you can't put the wrong fuel in your car and expect it to go very far because this will result mechanical problems, so how can you expect to put the wrong fuel (which your body wasn't designed for) inside your body? This fuel will have the same result in your body – diseases and pain.

If you are only starting with the raw food diet, rather than thinking of eating raw foods as the sole energy source, consider eating 80% raw, which will increase the chance for successful long-term raw eating. As mentioned before, lowering your intake of processed foods one food at a time, such as sugars, processed meats, enriched breads and foods with additives, can lead to long-term success with a raw vegan diet. If caffeine is consumed often, slowly reducing the intake will result in lessened caffeine withdrawal symptoms. During this time, slowly introduce new fruit and vegetable choices to aid in increased antioxidant intake thus detoxification in the body.

An effective strategy for eliminating processed foods and incorporating raw vegan foods is cleaning out the cupboards and replacing them with the following:

- Fresh fruit and vegetables

- Leafy greens

- Beans and legumes

- Whole grains – Quinoa, Buckwheat, Spelt Flour, Ezekiel Bread (for healthy cooked options in order to make an easier transition)

- Herbs – garlic, ginger, fresh parsley and basil

- Nuts and seeds

- Sweeteners – Raw Organic Dates Honey

- Super Foods – Maca Powder, Goji Berries, Spirulina.

Some quick examples of raw ingredient meal and snack ideas that help for an easier transition are:

- Leafy greens – lettuce, spinach, arugula, kale, cilantro, parsley, dill, Collards, basil, Cabbage.

- Sprouts – Mung, Adzuki, lentils, chickpea, pea, alfalfa, broccoli, radish, Mustard, Fenugreek.

- Fresh fruit – berries, banana, peach, apple, pineapple, watermelon, grapes, oranges, persimmon, apricot, pomegranate, pears, etc.

- Fresh vegetables – squash, peppers (variety), broccoli, cauliflower, carrot, etc.

- Healthy cooked choices – steamed vegetables, sweet potato, legumes and beans.

- Nuts and Seeds – Walnuts, almonds, sunflower seeds, pumpkin seeds, pecan, brazil nut, macadamia, hazel nut

- Dried fruit – Raisins, dates, apples, others without added sugar. (Make sure to buy them organic)

Making a list of the categories to start with and then slowly adding in more may also help with easier transition to a raw food lifestyle. Keep a diary and track everything - what you like, how you feel, what changes you see in your health, your body, your mind. So many people have seen great changes in their body when they moved to a raw vegan diet, be it: skin, eyesight, cancer, diabetes, ADHD, arthritis, mouth and teeth problems, body odor, osteoporosis, thyroid issues, liver, and list goes on.

Bonus: Get A FREE E-book & A Lot Of Valuable Information:

**Get "Training Motivation: How To Stop Making Excuses And
Increase Motivation To Exercise" Here:**

http://bit.ly/1DCZSfe

Conclusion

Thank you again for downloading this book!

As a parting shot, I would like to remind you that your body is a temple and you should treat it in a way that makes it the perfect picture of health and wellness.

I hope this book was able to help you learn what your body needs to be bursting with lean muscle.

The next step is to put all you have learnt in practice. Remember nothing comes easy and ***NO PAIN NO GAIN!***

Finally, if you enjoyed this book, please take the time to share your thoughts and post a review on Amazon. It'd be greatly appreciated!

Thank you and good luck!

Would you please leave a review?
Thank you!

Check Out My Other Books

Below you'll find some of my other popular books that are popular on Amazon and Kindle as well. Simply search their name on Amazon. Alternatively, you can visit my author page on Amazon to see other work done by me.

Food Addiction: How To Develop Self Discipline, Control Your Eating And Overcome Food Addiction

Vegan Kids Box Set: Vegan Recipes For Kids & Vegan Diet For Kids

Anti Aging From Within: How to Beat Your Aging Cells, Regenerate, Look Younger and Have Glowing, Vital Skin Naturally and Economically

Childhood Obesity: How To Help Your Child Achieve A Healthy Weight And Become Confident

Throw Away Your Asthma Inhaler: How To treat and beat Asthma Forever

You can simply search for these titles on the Amazon website to find them.